A Report to the Nation

The National Agenda for the Education of Children and Youths with Visual Impairments, Including Those with Multiple Disabilities

Editors
Anne L. Corn, Ed.D.
Kathleen Mary Huebner, Ph.D.

PRESS

New York

Printed in the United States of America

Library of Congress Cataloging-in-Publication Data

A report to the nation: the national agenda for the education of
    children and youths with visual impairments, including those with
    multiple disabilities / Anne L. Corn and Kathleen Mary Huebner,
    editors.
        p.   cm.
    Includes bibliographical references.
    ISBN 0-89128-319-6 (pbk.)
    1. Visually handicapped children—Education—United States.
2. Children, Blind—Education—United States. I. Corn, Anne
Lesley. II. Huebner, Kathleen Mary.
    HV1626.R48   1998
    371.91′1′0973—dc21   98-13630
                                                                          CIP

ISBN 0-89128-319-6 (alk. paper)

All the icons for each goal were designed by Erin Flaherty.

The mission of the American Foundation for the Blind (AFB) is to enable persons who are blind or visually impaired to achieve equality of access and opportunity that will ensure freedom of choice in their lives.

CONTENTS

PREFACE

A Parent's Perspective

"I can't see the stars the way you do, Dad, so you know what I do? I see them in my mind." My nine-year-old son with optic nerve hypoplasia said this to me one evening under a brilliant night sky. The air was crisp and the night very dark; in short, the perfect conditions to stargaze.

As in the past, I was once again reminded of difference. I was also reminded of the significance of perception, adaptation, compensation, creativity, innovation, and uniqueness. Difference can remind us of many good things; however, difference can also challenge us. All across the United States, children with visual impairments, including those with multiple disabilities, are entitled to the same educational rights through the Individuals with Disabilities Education Act (IDEA). This law governs special education, maps out specific policies and procedures, details educator and school-district responsibilities, and protects the rights of children with disabilities and their parents. For some children in the United States, this law has provided the framework for a superior educational experience. Braille instruction from a qualified teacher; orientation and mobility training from a certified teacher; rehabilitation services that are age appropriate; substantial, thorough, and timely technology and education assessments; parent involvement at every level; and other relevant services are the cornerstone of educational progress for these children.

But for other children in this country, a different scenario takes place. Some children who are totally blind do not have a teacher of braille. Can you imagine a sighted child not having a reading teacher? Some students who are visually impaired do not have instruction in orientation or mobility, including the use of canes and optical devices that enable children to move independently in their environments. Picture a sighted child who was not told what bus to take, what room to report to, or what stairway was where. Furthermore, some children with visual impairments have additional disabilities, but fail to receive adequate help for their visual disabilities because they are somehow deemed less important in contrast to their other challenges. Can you imagine how sighted children with diabetes, epilepsy, or Down syndrome must have felt around the turn of the century when their "disabilities" were the only factor recognized? In days of old, "difference" was synonymous with "less than."

The National Agenda asserts a concrete way to deal with an important difference for our children—visual impairments. When I consider how often I rely on my vision during the course of a normal day, I need only close one or both of my eyes, turn out an important light, or try to find an alternative to my car, pen, appointment book, or mirror. I do not have a visual impairment; I can only try to imagine what it is like to have one. Vision is a very precious commodity. The ability to see allows for various types of incidental learning that many of us take for granted. Children who are blind or visually impaired see differently than their sighted peers and, therefore, need to be educated to take that difference into account. If anyone has any doubt of this, just blindfold that person and try to teach that person something new. Educators need the appropriate tools, time, and talent to help these children learn to see in lieu of what their eyes are able to accomplish.

My son, Corbbmacc, needs a vision teacher to help him adapt to a regular classroom environment and learn what his peers are learning. He needs an orientation and mobility instructor to learn to navigate in unfamiliar environments so that he can be independent and productive. He requires technology to read what is too small or too far away. In addition, he participates in an adaptive physical education program so that he can compete, have fun, and enjoy his talents. Ultimately, my son uses his special education resources in order to begin the processes of competing, cooperating, computing, and comprehending. His peers learned these processes in large part by observation. We all adapt, but we all do so "differently." My eyeglasses are different from yours; imagine life without your personal prescription. My computer has a unique configuration of software, as does yours; imagine being forced to use mine alone for all of your personal applications.

It is how we deal with difference—constructing effective and creative adaptations for our children with visual impairments—that is the key challenge outlined in the National Agenda. The Agenda addresses the crucial issues of identification, equal parent participation, personnel preparation, ongoing professional development, specialized services, materials, individualized planning, and an array of placement options, which are the heart and soul of all good educational systems. All children have a legal and moral right to these educational services. The National Agenda is a call to make certain that those children do, in fact, receive these services as part of their educational day. As in many other areas of life, *saying* what should be and *doing* what should be are not always what *is*.

The eight goals of the National Agenda can only be accomplished through the combined effort of us all. When we close our eyes and envision what we want in our mind's eye, great things will happen for our children and youths. Only then can we take the creative, innovative, and courageous steps that are a part of every successful adaptation in life to deal effectively with change and difference.

As a parent, I know that visual impairment is not the only entity that can "blind." Judgments, prejudices, personal agendas, old ideas, misconceptions, inaccurate conclusions, and unwarranted anticipations will also blind us to what can be done or, more important, what *must* be done. Relying solely on the law can be another blinding problem as well. Progress is the result of people's efforts. Margaret Mead wrote, "Never doubt that a small group of thoughtful, committed people can change the world. Indeed, it is the only thing that ever has." The National Agenda and this *Report to the Nation* are positive steps toward fully implementing what each of us holds as a most treasured right: the right to learn.

Oliver Wendell Holmes remarked, "What lies behind us and what lies before us are tiny matters compared to what lies within us." During that clear, starry night, I learned something from my son that I believe exists within each one of us, if only we will close our eyes and see.

Kevin E. O'Connor
Immediate Past President
National Association for Parents of the
Visually Impaired (NAPVI)

A Professional's Perspective

Within a single year, 1832–33, three residential schools for the blind were opened in this country—in New York, Boston, and Philadelphia—and, by the Civil War, eighteen more were added. By the turn of the century, another 37 joined the list, and an additional dozen were established during the next two decades. Of the 55 residential schools in existence by 1972, only one was *less* than a century old.

These numbers testify to the fact that the United States has a long and successful history of pro-viding educational services to children who are blind. But a most fundamental change affecting the educational programs began when Chicago's first class for blind children in a regular public school was opened in September 1900. It did not take long for the Chicago formula to be tried elsewhere, countering the belief that blind and sighted children could not be schooled together and changing the numbers of blind children educated at residental schools to less than half of previous levels. This new model of public school education or integration of blind students in their local neighborhood schools was therefore in place when in 1975 the Education for All Handicapped Children Act was passed and the era of mainstreaming began in earnest.

Because of the mainstreaming of *all* children with disabilities, the cost of special education skyrocketed without the necessary federal funds to support it. Blind and visually impaired students, always a proportionately small population, were no longer primarily served in geographically concentrated locations, where services could be grouped effectively to meet unique but not dissimilar needs. Now a student body representing no more than 1 percent of the entire school-age population in the United States requires the delivery of unique educational services to small numbers spread geographically over a large and diverse country. At present the vast majority of blind children, some 90 percent (at least half of whom have multiple impairments), are mainstreamed in the regular public schools. This dramatic shift has demanded a large amount of financial and human resources. By the 1990s, the concept of mainstreaming began to change dramatically, with parents of disabled children demanding that their children spend a greater degree of time with their regular school classmates. Thus, the concept of inclusion began, demanding the placement of disabled children, including those who are blind, in regular classroom settings at all costs, often without the necessary support of specialized teachers.

What has been the result? A decline in the adequacy of services received. From the 1970s on, the race for the special education dollar has become so competitive that local educational agencies have been forced to make decisions based on financial resources rather than students' needs. It is expensive to educate visually impaired children by virtue of their unique needs and low prevalence. And the elevation of inclusion as a preeminent goal has often eroded the provision of important support services needed by children in a regular school setting. Some people have called into question the viability of placement in and costs of residential schools, without understanding the need for a continuum of placement options, including the choice of residential school settings for some children at particular points of time in their education. However, the availability of a variety of placement options and of a continuum of services helps ensure the most supportive learning environment with appropriately trained teachers to meet individual needs rather than administrative mandates.

What has all this to do with the National Agenda? It is the National Agenda and this *Report to the Nation* that document what we already knew—that blind children are not receiving the quantity or quality of educational services they need. The documented evidence contained in the data and reports presented in the following pages stand as a hallmark of what our nation's blind children deserve and need in order to achieve their highest potential. If the areas of assessment, prompt referrals to a full array of appropriate services, training of teachers, parent participation, and individualized programming are to be addressed, this publication is a testament that can be cited, a rallying point around which to organize, and a map that can be used to chart remedial action.

We have seen the educational impact, over the years, of the changing service delivery model from only one school setting serving all blind children to all schools serving blind children. But this movement toward mainstreaming can only be successful if we keep in mind the actual learning needs of the students involved and separate them from theoretical rhetoric. The National Agenda has set the goals showing how this can happen and offers the tools to pave the way.

SUSAN JAY SPUNGIN, Ed.D.
Vice President, National Programs
American Foundation for the Blind

ACKNOWLEDGMENTS

On behalf of infants, toddlers, children, and youths who are blind or visually impaired, including those with multiple disabilities, we thank everyone who has been involved in the development and implementation of the National Agenda. Because it is typical of individuals concerned with the education of children who are blind or visually impaired, we have grown to expect cooperation and quality of effort. But never did we expect so many people to be committed to putting their creative thoughts and hands to implementing the National Agenda. It is impossible to list everyone from the many early intervention programs, schools, and organizations of professionals, parents, and consumers at local, state, and national levels who have shared in this effort. Families, teachers, orientation and mobility instructors, students, administrators, and other service providers are pulling together to achieve the National Agenda's eight goals throughout the nation. This report presents only a portion of their combined efforts.

We express a special thanks to the National Goal Leaders, State Coordinators, and Advisory Board members for their written contributions to this *Report to the Nation*. They have worked tirelessly to establish baseline data, develop and implement local or state action plans, conduct research to prepare informative reports, and respond and contribute whenever asked. Readers will benefit from their reports by being able to use the information for furthering their own efforts at advocacy and policy development.

We thank the schools, organizations, and agencies who have both endorsed the National Agenda and supported efforts to achieve it by providing staff time and other resources. Foundations and others have contributed toward the funding of research efforts and dissemination of information. Special recognition is extended to the American Foundation for the Blind and the American Printing House for the Blind for providing national forums in which strategies to meet the goals could be developed.

We would especially like to recognize the tireless efforts of Frank Ryan and Mary Ann Siller, National Program Associates in Education for the American Foundation for the Blind. Erin Flaherty, a graduate of the Pennsylvania College of Optometry and an Orientation and Mobility Therapist with the New York City Board of Education, Education Vision Services, created the icons used to represent the concepts inherent in each of the eight National Agenda Goals.

Special thanks are extended to Traci Williams, Secretary for the Graduate Studies Department, Institute for the Visually Impaired, Pennsylvania College of Optometry. Traci used her skills and talents to pull together material originally submitted in many different formats. Thanks also go to Debbie Whelan, Secretary to the Program in Visual Disabilities at Peabody College, Vanderbilt University, for her tireless effort in preparing the manuscript for submission.

It is our hope this *Report to the Nation* serves as a banner for National Agenda efforts and progress to date and will provide motivation and encouragement for others to join a truly national movement toward improving educational opportunities for every infant, toddler, child, and youth who is blind or visually impaired.

ANNE L. CORN, Ed.D.
Professor of Special Education,
Ophthalmology and Visual Sciences,
Vanderbilt University
KATHLEEN MARY HUEBNER, Ph.D.
Assistant Dean, Graduate Studies
Pennsylvania College of Optometry

INTRODUCTION

The National Agenda will significantly improve educational services for blind and visually impaired students. Both its leadership and front-line workers consist of parents, professionals, and visually impaired persons—all dedicated to the achievement of the eight goals at the heart of the National Agenda. These goals have been widely acknowledged as the most critical issues confronting the quality of education for visually impaired children and youths.

Early in the planning stages, the need for state-of-the-art information on each of these goals was apparent. Progress toward achieving them would be impossible to measure without knowing the current status of services for blind and visually impaired students. A systematic approach to gathering such data was necessary since each goal identifies a specific issue. A first step was the careful selection of organizations to serve as National Goal Leaders (NGLs). Once selected, an individual within each NGL organization assumed primary responsibility for data collection and reporting. Collectively, the work of these organizations and individuals illuminates the current status of the National Agenda's eight goals. Presentations at conferences and meetings across the country have enabled parents, consumers, and professionals to become aware of the NGLs' commitment and the outstanding quality of their work. Through this *Report to the Nation,* the current status of the National Agenda is available to all.

From the outset, local schools, agencies, and organizations have been involved. It is here that achievement of the eight goals is going to occur for individual children and their families. Currently, 158 such schools, agencies, and vision-related organizations have endorsed the National Agenda and committed themselves to supporting efforts toward achieving those goals. With encouragement and enthusiastic leadership from State Coordinators and others, numerous grassroots efforts are underway to implement the National Agenda's eight goals on local and state levels. Many of these efforts are described in this *Report to the Nation.*

For many years, we have observed and participated in a variety of efforts to improve the quality of education for blind and visually impaired students. Nothing in which we have been involved holds the promise of the National Agenda. Never before have professionals, parents, and visually impaired persons been called on to collaborate on such a clearly defined task. We urge you to read this publication, consider the implications of the information presented, and commit yourselves to full achievement of the National Agenda's eight goals. Blind and visually impaired children are depending on you.

DONNA STRYKER
President
National Association for Parents of the Visually Impaired (NAPVI)
PHIL HATLEN
Superintendent
Texas School for the Blind and Visually Impaired
Co-chairs, National Agenda

OVERVIEW OF THE NATIONAL AGENDA

What Is the National Agenda?

The National Agenda is a set of priorities, stated as goals, that are ever present in the minds of parents, professionals, and persons with visual impairments—individuals with personal or professional interests in educational services and opportunities provided for children and youths with visual impairments. The National Agenda was crafted as a means by which significant improvements can occur in the quality and nature of educational services and programs for infants, toddlers, children, and youths who are blind or have low vision, with or without additional disabilities. It is truly "national" in scope. From Maine to California and Alaska to Florida, parents, professionals, and persons with visual impairments are working together. Their shared objective is the enactment of changes that have been identified as not only the most needed but also having the greatest potential for positively impacting how we, as a nation, educate and work with children with visual impairments and their families. As an "agenda," we must remain focused on these priorities until they have been achieved, ideally within the next few years.

What Are the Goals of the National Agenda?

The following goal statements apply to infants, toddlers, children, and youths with visual impairments, including those with multiple disabilities.

Goal 1.

Students and their families will be referred to an appropriate education program within thirty days of identification of a suspected visual impairment.

Goal 2.

Policies and procedures will be implemented to ensure the right of all parents to full participation and equal partnership in the education process.

Goal 3.

Universities, with a minimum of one full-time faculty member in the area of visual impairment, will prepare a sufficient number of educators of students with visual impairments to meet personnel needs throughout the country.

Goal 4.

Service providers will determine caseloads based on the needs of students and will require ongoing professional development for all teachers and orientation and mobility instructors.

Goal 5.

Local education programs will ensure that all students have access to a full array of placement options.

Goal 6.

Assessment of students will be conducted, in collaboration with parents, by personnel having expertise in the education of students with visual impairments.

Goal 7.

Access to developmental and educational services will include an assurance that instructional materials are available to students in the appropriate media and at the same time as their sighted peers.

Goal 8.

Educational and developmental goals, including instruction, will reflect the assessed needs of each student in all areas of academic and disability-specific core curricula.

What Does the National Agenda Mean for Children and Youths with Visual Impairments and Their Families?

Never before have so many segments of our population collaborated on such a grand scale to achieve educational changes for a group of infants, toddlers, children, and youths with a common disability. Never before have parents of children with visual impairments and professionals come together, working as equal partners, to achieve what neither group could accomplish alone. Never before have adults with visual disabilities been called on in such a meaningful way to have direct input into educational opportunities for the next generation of children experiencing what they did as students in public day and specialized schools. The National Agenda is a living, dynamic, energizing document. All involved in working to achieve its

goals have a mission, one that they share with all who have a personal or professional interest in providing appropriate educational opportunities for children and youths with visual impairments.

The National Agenda means different things to different people. At its heart are infants, toddlers, children, youths with impaired or no sight, and their families. From that point on they are as diverse as the population at large. As a result of their visual impairment, they have unique educational needs requiring specialized teaching strategies and materials. These are essential if they are to fully benefit from educational opportunities considered to be a right in this country. Because of their uniqueness, both as children with visual impairments and as individuals, the National Agenda takes on different meanings as it applies to each child. The family, school, and community must respond to and provide for each child's individual educational needs in order to facilitate his or her growth and development.

To parents, the National Agenda empowers them to strive for significant changes on behalf of their visually impaired children and in concert with educators. The parent-professional partnership, inherent in the agenda and its processes, confirms that they are full participants in their children's education. To professionals, the National Agenda is a method of gathering forces to bring about needed changes and improvements not just for their own students, but for all students with visual impairments. Adults with visual impairments are truly the "experts" at being visually impaired. For them, the National Agenda confirms that their contributions are welcomed and necessary. As parents, professionals, and persons with visual impairments share their common interests, needs, insights, and strategies, the National Agenda has become a unifying force, a communication link, and an empowering document.

Who Developed the National Agenda?

From its origins to its current structure, the National Agenda is truly a grass-roots effort. Parents, professionals, and persons with visual impairments all have shared roles, responsibilities, and commitments. No single individual, school, or organization created the National Agenda nor directs its course for achieving its goals for our nation. All had a stake in its development. Each takes from it those goals that will improve educational services throughout the country and incorporates what may be unique to his or her state, agency, or school. Individuals and groups have responded to, built on, or structured their personal National Agenda efforts in response to the strengths, weaknesses, needs, and challenges of their state or region. A strategy for collaborating with schools in Arkansas may not be appropriate in Ohio or California. Successful strategies for improving collaboration between parents and medical personnel or teachers in Utah may differ greatly from those that work in Mississippi or New York. Although sharing a common mission, each entity brings to the National Agenda a history and culture unique in many ways.

How Is the National Agenda Organized?

The National Agenda is co-chaired by Ms. Donna Stryker, a parent from New Mexico, and Dr. Phil Hatlen, a professional from Texas. The Advisory Board includes the original steering committee plus additional parents, professionals, and adults with visual impairments from throughout the United States. National Goal Leaders (NGLs) are organizations, agencies, and schools that have committed to helping the nation achieve one of the Agenda's eight goals. Working individually or in teams, professionals and parents also serve as state coordinators, pursuing achievement of the goals within their respective states. In many states, teams consisting of parents, professionals, and consumers are working to make the benefits of the National Agenda a reality for their children and students at the local level. More than 150 public and private agencies, organizations, and schools have endorsed the National Agenda. Their endorsement is much more than mere approval of its process and goals. Each has committed resources toward achieving the National Agenda within the context of services they provide to or on behalf of children and their families.

Why Was the National Agenda Developed?

The National Agenda came about because of an acknowledgment that children and youths with visual impairments are not consistently or universally receiving the quantity or quality of educational services appropriate for their special learning needs. Clearly, all was not right with the educational serv-

ices being provided. The following deficiencies are but a few of the many that could be cited as examples.

Many students do not receive services from teachers specially trained in the area of visual impairments or O&M (orientation and mobility) instruction.

Brailled textbooks too often do not arrive in a timely manner (i.e., at the same time sighted classmates receive books in print).

Assessments frequently are conducted by professionals lacking knowledge of the learning implications of being blind.

Lack of low-tech devices and training in their use prevent students with low vision from viewing chalkboards.

The net result of these and other shortcomings is that far too many students who are blind or have low vision graduate from high school lacking the skills or emotional preparedness essential for gainful employment or leading more rewarding, enjoyable adult lives.

Among parents and professionals a level of discontent with the "status quo" had grown to the point where something had to be done. Collectively, educators, parents, and persons with visual impairments have the power to create the needed changes. Through the joint efforts of all involved with the National Agenda, every visually impaired child can be empowered to take his or her rightful place in society as a contributing member of family and community.

How Was the National Agenda Established?

Before a discussion of how the National Agenda came about, let us offer a brief explanation of the structure of the major gatherings of professionals and parents. It was through these established means for communication that the idea for a National Agenda was discussed, developed, and planned.

Each fall the American Printing House for the Blind (APH), a leading national developer and distributor of educational materials for children and youths who are visually impaired, holds an annual meeting. Each spring the American Foundation for the Blind (AFB), a national organization working toward equality of opportunities for all persons with visual disabilities, holds the Josephine L.

Taylor Leadership Institute (JLTLI). These annual meetings provide a forum for APH Trustees, superintendents of special schools, leaders of major parent and consumer organizations, directors of instructional materials resource centers, supervisors of public school programs, and others to share and learn about new products, services, and legislative or policy matters. Discussions focus on national challenges and issues in the field of blindness and visual impairments with participants working in groups to address them. Every two years the Association for Education and Rehabilitation of the Blind and Visually Impaired (AER), the largest professional organization in this field, holds an international conference.

At the 1993 APH Trustees Meeting, a brief speech titled "The Challenges We Face," implying that all is right in the nation, was delivered as a satire. The speaker, Dr. Anne L. Corn, stated that reading levels and speeds of students with visual impairments approximated those of normally sighted students, that employment levels of graduates were at levels comparable to those without disabilities, and so forth. Following this presentation, a small group of professionals challenged their peers to identify national goals leading to the actualization that "all is right in the nation."

Other national education efforts were underway as well. The 1990 report, *A Nation at Risk,* had alerted America to problems in our nation's schools at large. This led to the movement known as Goals 2000, which stipulated goals for improving education for all children in the United States. Goals 2000 addressed education in general, but did not specifically address the needs of children with disabilities. In response, another effort by the U.S. Office for Special Education resulted in a document, *Achieving Better Results for Children with Disabilities.* This spoke of changes needed in special education, but did not include the needs of children who are blind or have low vision. Some parents and professionals in the field of blindness and visual impairments voiced concern that a separate agenda for students with visual impairments might segregate them from children with other disabilities or with no disabilities. Although short-lived, these discussions made it clear that we needed to get our "own house in order." Only then could we set out to effect changes in such areas as a core

curriculum for students with visual disabilities as well as address other instructional priorities essential for the education of children who are blind or have low vision.

In January 1994, an open letter appeared in several blindness-related journals and newsletters, proposing a National Agenda specific to children and youths with visual impairments. From throughout the United States a resounding "yes" was heard. At the next JLTLI, work groups, tailored according to the categories of responses received to the open letter, initiated the process of identifying goals for a National Agenda. These JLTLI participants wisely determined that the involvement of additional parents, professionals, and persons with visual impairments was needed. Each work group elected a chair to continue its work beyond JLTLI. These committees and their chairs were Ms. Mardi Roberts, Initial Referral and Assessment; Dr. Phil Hatlen, Educational Curriculum Needs; Mr. Kevin O'Connor, Services to Meet Needs; Dr. Brian McCartney, Transition and Postsecondary Outcomes; and Dr. Jane Erin, Preparation and Availability of Personnel.

With Dr. Anne L. Corn, a professional and an adult with a visual impairment, as its chair, the National Agenda Steering Committee was established. Other members included Dr. Kathleen M. Huebner, Dr. Phil Hatlen, Ms. Mary Ann Siller, and Mr. Frank Ryan. Adding other members, this committee later evolved into a standing National Agenda Advisory Board. The Steering Committee suggested that each of the five work groups recommend three to five goals specific to their categorical area. Each proposed goal should meet two criteria: namely, if achieved, it would have major positive impact on the education of children and youths with visual impairments, and could be achievable by the year 2000. Nineteen goal statements, deemed to meet these criteria, were submitted to the Steering Committee.

Employing a Likelihood-Impact Analysis process, the most critical goals were identified, thereby establishing a realistic number on which to focus. This had the added benefit of involving many additional parents, professionals, and persons with visual impairments. Using a Likert-type five-point scale, respondents were asked to review each proposed goal statement and rate the extent of its potential impact on educational services and programs. Each respondent was also asked to use a similar scale to indicate his or her belief in how likely the goal could be achieved by the year 2000. More than two thousand surveys were distributed throughout the United States. Five hundred and sixteen completed forms were received representing parents, professionals, and persons with visual impairments in forty states. Dr. Virginia Bishop analyzed the data and forwarded it to the Steering Committee. This information enabled the Steering Committee to identify the eight goals with the highest likelihood of achievement and greatest potential for positive impact. At the 1994 AER Conference, the eight goal statements were read and discussed by the AER divisions that have direct relevance to the education of children and youth with visual impairments. This provided additional input from the field that assisted the Steering Committee in a final editing of the goal statements for purposes of clarity.

By September 1994, the eight goals of the National Agenda were established and the strategies needed to achieve them were developed. Major organizations and schools, each with expertise and resources specific to one of the goal areas, were asked to volunteer to serve as National Goal Leaders (NGLs). Eight organizations of national leadership stature immediately volunteered.

In October 1995, the National Agenda was finalized and presented at the APH meeting as a booklet published by AFB Press and authored by the original steering committee. The Advisory Board selected co-chairs. Confirming the parent-professional partnership evident throughout the National Agenda, Donna Stryker, a parent, and Phil Hatlen, a professional, were selected. State Coordinators were also selected to serve as key contacts and liaisons for the National Agenda within each state.

In July 1996, two articles appeared in *RE:view,* a journal for professionals in this field. One documented the development of the National Agenda and the data that compelled the Steering Committee to identify the eight goals. The second article specifically addressed Goal 8, the core curriculum. It is believed that ultimately, if each goal is achieved, and if the core curriculum is made available to all children and youth with visual impairments, then equality of educational opportunity will be within reach.

The Nation Embraces the National Agenda

Over the past three years, the National Agenda has been the subject of numerous presentations delivered at state, national, and international meetings of parents, professionals, and persons with visual impairments. For three years the JLTLI has identified work on the National Agenda as the primary focus of its Education Work Group. By 1998, nearly two hundred organizations, representing hundreds of thousands of individuals, have endorsed the National Agenda. Countless individuals and organizations continue to support the effort through time, energy, commitment, and other resources. National Agenda public information packets, consisting of a copy of the National Agenda booklet and other supporting materials, have received widespread distribution. Multiple copies of the packets were sent to all state coordinators, NGLs, and other interested individuals.

As the National Agenda effort became a reality, each NGL agreed to gather data during the first year to determine how close or how far the nation is from reaching the goal. The data obtained provide a quantifiable base of information. The next sections of this report contain the eight goals and the data obtained by the NGLs.

Who Are the NGLs?

Goal 1: *Referral:* Students and their families will be referred to an appropriate education program within thirty days of identification of a suspected visual impairment. NGL—Foundation for Blind Children, Arizona

Goal 2: *Parent Participation:* Policies and procedures will be implemented to ensure the right of all parents to full participation and equal partnership in the education process. NGL—National Association for Parents of the Visually Impaired

Goal 3: *Personnel Preparation:* Universities, with a minimum of one full-time faculty member in the area of visual impairment, will prepare a sufficient number of educators of students with visual impairments to meet personnel needs throughout the country. NGL—AER Division 17

Goal 4: *Provision of Educational Services:* Service providers will determine caseloads based on the needs of students and will require ongoing professional development for all teachers and orientation and mobility instructors. NGL—Association of State Educational Consultants for the Visually Impaired

Goal 5: *Array of Services:* Local education programs will ensure that all students have access to a full array of placement options. NGL—Council of Schools for the Blind

Goal 6: *Assessment:* Assessment of students will be conducted, in collaboration with parents, by personnel having expertise in the education of students with visual impairments. NGL—Lighthouse National Center for Vision and Child Development, The Lighthouse Inc.

Goal 7: *Access to Instructional Materials:* Access to developmental and educational services will include an assurance that instructional materials are available to students in the appropriate media and at the same time as their sighted peers. NGL—Association of Instructional Resource Centers for the Visually Handicapped

Goal 8: *Core Curriculum:* Educational and developmental goals, including instruction, will reflect the assessed needs of each student in all areas of academic and disability-specific core curricula. NGL—Texas School for the Blind and Visually Impaired

NATIONAL GOAL REPORTS

A major charge to the National Goal Leaders (NGLs) was to gather national data that would provide information about the current status of each goal. Although the goal statements were based on experiences and beliefs, there was a need to know how well we as a nation were faring on each. Data gathered by the NGLs would offer a national "snapshot" to serve as a benchmark from which states, local schools, and organizations could determine how well their services compared to the nation as a whole. As of this writing, several studies are being used to guide action plans and other studies are still underway.

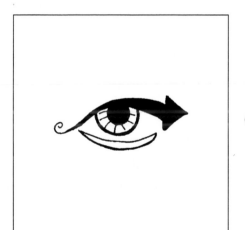

Goal 1

Students and their families will be referred to an appropriate education program within thirty days of identification of a suspected visual impairment.

Submitted by the Foundation for Blind Children, Phoenix, Arizona
Prepared by Chris Tompkins, Executive Director

Background

Visually impaired children have unique educational and developmental needs. Vision is the primary way sighted children receive and process information. This is especially true for very young children, for whom visual learning and imitation are the keys to early development. For the young visually impaired child, and that child's family, it is especially important that referrals be made as soon after diagnosis as possible to facilitate early educational and developmental services. These services teach children adaptive ways of learning about the world around them and how to compensate for the loss of vision in gathering, processing, and understanding that world. It is critical that parents receive early intervention so that they may learn the impact of vision loss on early development and how to teach their child adaptively. The key to successful development is early professional intervention services, and the key to early services is prompt referral after diagnosis.

Procedure

A parent questionnaire was developed to assess the current status of time between diagnosis of visual impairment and referral for early intervention services. It was written with input from teachers, counselors, early interventionists, and parents throughout the country. The final product consisted of thirteen questions eliciting demographic, diagnostic, and service and referral information. A copy of the questionnaire is shown in Figure 1. Two hundred and thirty-nine families from 27 states responded. The following is an analysis of their responses.

Analysis of Time Lapse Between Diagnosis and Referral for Early Intervention Services

N—239 Respondents		Responses from 27 States (11% Return on Surveys Mailed)	
Community		Birth Year	
Urban	30%	1993–96	63%
Suburban	54%	1990–92	37%
Rural	16%		
Eye Condition		Other Disability	65% yes
Cortical Visual Impairment (CVI)	22%	Cerebral Palsy (CP)	36%
Retinopathy of Prematurity (ROP)	13%	Developmental Delay	23%
Optic Nerve Hypoplasia	10%	Hydrocephalus	8%
Coloboma	6%	Microcephalus	3%
Retinoschisis/PHPV	6%	Seizure Disorder	3%
Cataracts	5%	Down Syndrome	3%
Albinism	5%	Charge Syndrome	2%
Micro Ophthalmia	4%	Other Categories	22%
Myopia/Hyperopia	3%		
Anophthalmia	2%		
Leber's	2%		
Optic Atrophy	2%		
Glaucoma	2%		
Other Categories	18%		

How old was your child when diagnosed?

Age In Months	
6	79%
12	92%
24	98%

How old was your child when you were first told about special education/early intervention?

Age In Months	
6	71%
12	85%
24	97%

Were you provided with an understandable explanation of the kinds of early intervention services available to you and anticipated outcomes of early intervention?

Yes	82%
No	18%

How old was your child when s/he was first enrolled in a special education/early intervention program?

Age In Months When Enrolled	
6	52%
12	77%
24	90%
36	94%

Did your child's early intervention program address your child's needs with respect to blindness and visual impairment?

Yes   73%
No   23%
Not enrolled   4%

Who first diagnosed your child's visual impairment?

Ophthalmologist   49%
Pediatrician   19%
Neurologist   13%
Other   19%

Who first told you about early intervention?

Educator/Agency Counselor   26%
Ophthalmologist   24%
Pediatrician   7%
Neurologist   5%
Nurse   6%
Others   32%

Discussion of Findings

1. The results show a fairly predictable distribution of families across urban, suburban, and rural settings. In the comments from the family section of the questionnaire, rural families more frequently identified needs for earlier referral and better services.

2. The incidence of eye conditions in this sample shows cortical visual impairment as the most common condition, followed by retinopathy of prematurity (ROP) and optic nerve hypoplasia. In addition, 65 percent of the sample were children with additional disabilities.

3. Seventy-nine percent of children were diagnosed by the age of six months and 92 percent by twelve months. Given the critical role of vision in early learning, it seems important to address those children not diagnosed before six and twelve months.

4. Seventy-one percent of the sample was told about special education or early intervention services by the age of six months and 85 percent by twelve months. This is a good start and a respectable number. However, the primary recommendation by parents on how to improve the referral process was to have an information system in the medical community that results in earlier referral and more information about available resources.

5. Eighty-two percent of the sample were provided with understandable explanations of both the kinds of early intervention services available and their anticipated outcomes. Eighteen percent of the sample were not.

6. Fifty-two percent of the children in the sample were enrolled in special education early intervention programs by the age of six months. That increased to 77 percent by the age of twelve months and 94 percent by the age of three. Once again, given the critical importance of early educational and developmental intervention for both child and family, a significant number of children and families in the sample did not receive early services.

7. Seventy-three percent of the early intervention services specifically addressed needs with regard to blindness and visual impairment and 23 percent did not. Given the unique role of vision in early learning and the individual education and developmental needs of the blind or visually impaired child, this result may suggest a need to look at early intervention program requirements for expertise in blindness and visual impairments.

8. Forty-nine percent of the children were diagnosed by ophthalmologists and 51 percent by others from the medical community (i.e., pediatricians and neurologists). The diversity of the response to who first diagnosed the child's visual

impairment underscores the importance of focusing on the broad medical community, not just ophthalmology.

9. The responses to question 12 regarding who first told the family about early intervention services was apparently misleading and confusing to families because the leading response was the educator or early interventionist. Obviously, in most cases, the family was given a prior referral to that service provider.

Recommendations

The parents in the sample had two primary recommendations:

1. Medical doctors need more information on early referral and intervention and must make referrals sooner and more often. There was a sense on the part of some parents that doctors do not understand or believe in the importance of early intervention services.
2. Personnel including nurses and social workers in doctors' offices, hospitals, and specialty clinics need information on local/regional programs and resources so they can make early and better referrals.

A group of doctors from throughout the country who actively make early referrals were asked for recommendations on how to improve the process. They had two primary recommendations:

1. Develop simple handouts on local/regional services that can be broadly distributed to the medical community.
2. Involve the medical community with local/regional special education early service intervention systems through advisory boards and as resources for in-service training. In this way doctors and other medical service providers can have firsthand knowledge of early intervention special education programs and thus formulate collaborative relationships.

The final recommendation is to utilize this data together with the knowledge we as professionals and parents have concerning the importance of and need for prompt referral for special education early intervention services for developing a detailed plan of action that will enable this nation to reach the first goal of this National Agenda.

That is our challenge and our opportunity. Surely we can do no less.

Dear Parents:

The following questionnaire has been designed to determine at what age visually impaired or blind children are being diagnosed, referred for services, and receiving services. It is being collected by the Steering Committee of the National Agenda for the Education of Children and Youth with Visual Impairments, Including those with Multiple Disabilities. The information you provide will be used to plan ways to achieve the following goal: "Students and their families will be referred to an appropriate education program within thirty days of identification of a suspected visual impairment."

If you are the parent of a child who has been diagnosed as blind or visually impaired in the past five years, won't you please take a moment to fill out the following information? Thank you in advance for your help.

Sincerely,

Chris Tompkins, National Goal Leader
Foundation for Blind Children, Phoenix, Arizona

- -

Please return the questionnaire to: Dr. Jane Erin, University of Arizona, College of Education, Department of Special Education and Rehabilitation, Tucson, Arizona 85721.

1. In what state do you live? _____

2. In what type of area do you live?

   Urban _____   Suburban _____   Rural _____

3. What is your child's birth date?

   Mo. _____   Day _____   Yr. _____

4. What is your child's eye condition?

   _____

5. Does she/he have other disabilities or health concerns? Please describe.

   _____

   _____

   _____

6. Who first diagnosed your child's visual impairment?

   _____ Pediatrician   _____ Optometrist   _____ Neurologist

   _____ Ophthalmologist   _____ Nurse   _____ Educator

   _____ Other _____

7. How old was your child when diagnosed? _____

8. How old was your child when you were first told about special education/early interventions? _____

9. Were you provided with an understandable explanation of the kinds of early intervention services available to you

   and the anticipated outcomes of early interventions? _____

10. How old was your child when she/he was first enrolled in a special education/early intervention program? _____

11. Did your child's early intervention program address your child's needs with respect to blindness and visual

    impairment? _____

12. Who first told you about services for your visually impaired child? [see the list in #6] _____

13. How do you think the referral process could have been improved for you and your child? _____

    _____

Comments: _____

_____

Optional: Name _____

            Phone _____

            Address _____

Figure 1.   Parent Questionnaire.

Goal 2

Policies and procedures will be implemented to ensure the right of all parents to full participation and equal partnership in the education process.

Submitted by the National Association for Parents of the Visually Impaired
Prepared by Susan LaVenture

Background

The Individuals with Disabilities Education Act (IDEA), formerly known as the Education for All Handicapped Children Act (EHA), is the federal law supporting special education and related services for students with disabilities. This law sets the course for the nation's educational system by stating the right of all students with disabilities, including those with visual impairments, to a free and appropriate education in the least restrictive environment. Parents were integral to the passage of the original legislation in 1975 and the subsequent legislation and regulations that frame special education today. Continued parental involvement at all levels in the education process is essential. Although all children have specific learning needs, children with a visual impairment have their own specific educational requirements.

IDEA ensures parent involvement through policies in the following areas: informed notice and consent, evaluation, individualized education programs, procedural due process, advisory panels to state agencies, and privacy of and access to student records. Parents are guaranteed the right to a full and equal participation in their children's education program. Parents who use the knowledge they have regarding their children's abilities and needs and employ advocacy skills in working with professionals can be highly effective in assuring an appropriate education program for their children. By knowing their child's abilities and disabilities and special education laws, parents can be effective communicators. The ability to demonstrate appropriate assertiveness is another trait that contributes to being a partner in the educational process.

The National Association for Parents of the Visually Impaired (NAPVI) has learned from the experiences of parents who too often encounter battles over what families see as the educational needs of their children and what the schools see or are able to provide. Several issues have emerged that are deeply troubling to parents. For example, a shortage of professionals trained to deliver disability-specific services—e.g., orientation and mobility, braille reading and writing and other adapted communication modes, and independent living skills—severely impacts the educational achievements of many blind children. NAPVI also has concerns that parents may not be told what constitutes an appropriate education for their children or that the services from specially trained teachers should be available.

NAPVI is leading the effort to ensure that all parents of children with visual impairments, including those with multiple disabilities, view themselves and are viewed by others as equal partners, fully participating in their children's education. This is the aim of the collaborative effort between parents and professionals, exemplified in the National Agenda.

Procedure

NAPVI's National Board of Directors developed a written survey to learn the extent to which parents are involved in the educational processes of their children. Board members who prepared the survey are parents of children with varying degrees of visual impairments ranging from total blindness to low vision. Some have mild to severe additional disabilities. The questionnaire reflected parents' experiences with their own children's education as well as those of hundreds of other families with whom they interact.

The survey was designed to measure how knowledgeable, comfortable, and involved parents are with education programs and services for children who are visually impaired. A five-point Likert-type scale was used. Six questions addressed parents' level of knowledge and eleven addressed their level of comfort.

Five questions, calling for a "yes" or "no" response, referred to involvement levels in educational processes in general and procedures related to Individual Education Programs (IEP) meetings. For any responses of "no," respondents were asked to state a reason. Two open-ended questions allow for comments about difficulties encountered with the educational process or system and for recommendations to help parents feel like more of a "partner" in their child's education.

Distribution of Surveys

Surveys were included as an insert in the Spring 1996 issue of *Awareness,* NAPVI's national membership newsletter. They were also distributed to parents at the Missouri Parent Professional Partnership Statewide Conference and to parents of children served by the Texas School for the Blind and Visually Impaired. Only parents of children who are visually impaired, including some with multiple disabilities, were asked to complete the survey.

Results

Completed surveys were received from 101 parents in the following eighteen states: California, Iowa, Kentucky, Maine, Massachusetts, New Hampshire, New York, Ohio, Pennsylvania, Missouri, Illinois, North Carolina, Georgia, Tennessee, Texas, Oregon, Vermont, and Wisconsin. Children in the responses were in grades K–12 from both rural and urban areas and a broad range of educational placements (i.e., special schools for the blind, local public and private schools). On a five-point Likert scale, the percentages of responses were examined for those who indicated knowledge and comfort levels in the two highest and two lowest ratings. Those who felt they were knowledgeable were expected to respond with 1s and 2s while those who felt little or no knowledge responded with 4s and 5s. It was assumed that those who responded with a 3 felt that they may have had some level of knowledge or comfort but not enough to rate a 1 or 2.

Table 1 shows by percentage the levels at which parents feel knowledgeable about the educational process for their children. Although 69 percent of the parents felt they were knowledgeable about their children's current abilities and 77 percent felt knowledgeable about their children's educational needs, only 50 percent indicated that they felt knowledgeable about their children's future potential. Parents expressed more confidence in the knowledge of professionals involved with their children; 79 percent of the parents indicated they felt professionals were knowledgeable about vision problems and their effects on learning. Similar percentages, 58 percent and 59 percent, felt knowledgeable about their legal rights and educational programs and services available for their own children, respectively. A slightly lower percentage, 48 percent, of the parents indicated they felt knowledgeable about the educational needs of students with visual impairments in general.

Table 2 summarizes parents' responses regarding their comfort levels. It uses a similar presentation of the percentages of parents' responses. Interestingly, 84 percent of parents indicated that they were comfortable meeting individually with professionals regarding their children. However, a lower percentage, 75 percent, felt comfortable discussing their concerns with professionals when they believed changes were needed in their children's program. A slightly lower number, 73 percent, indicated they were comfortable going to their child's IEP meetings. Only 65 percent felt comfortable voicing personal opinions when disagreements arise regarding their child's program. Seventy percent said they were comfortable with the process of finding solutions to problems concerning their children's programs.

Table 3 shows that 93 percent of the parents feel involved in their children's educational planning process. Forty-six percent indicated that everyone who provides services to their children was present at their last IEP meeting. Of parents indicating that some service providers were not present, 29 percent said they were given written progress reports by professionals not in attendance and 34 percent reported they were not. Overall, 70 percent stated they were given a written progress report at their children's last IEP meeting while 22 percent said they were not. Eight percent did not respond to this question.

Table 1 Parents' Levels of Knowledge Regarding Education Process for Children with Visual Impairments, Including Those with Multiple Disabilities, by Percent

	Most Knowledgeable			No Knowledge	
How knowledgeable do you feel about:	1	2	3	4	5
Your child's current abilities	44	25	29	2	1
Your child's future potential	19	31	26	11	6
The educational needs of your child	26	51	21	2	5
The educational needs of visually impaired children	16	32	38	9	5
Your legal rights as the parent of a child with vision problems	25	33	26	10	6
Educational programs and services available for your visually impaired child	20	30	29	9	2

Table 2 Parents' Levels of Comfort Regarding the Education Process for Children with Visual Impairments, Including Those with Multiple Disabilities, by Percent

	Most Comfortable			Not Comfortable	
How comfortable are you:	1	2	3	4	5
Going to your child's IEP/IFS meeting	47	26	17	6	4
Meeting individually with professionals (teachers, administrators, speech therapists, etc.) about your child's needs	57	27	12	1	2
Discussing your concerns with professionals about the need to change your child's program	46	29	27	5	4
Making suggestions about changes needed in the education program	43	26	14	7	1
Disagreeing with professionals involved in your child's program	38	27	15	10	1
Problem solving with professionals to find solutions	43	27	18	5	2

Table 3 Parents' Level of Involvement and Procedures Followed for IEP Meetings, by Percent

Question	Yes	Yes/No	No
Do you feel involved in your child's educational planning process?	93	2	3
Are the specialists involved with your child knowledgeable about vision problems and the effect on learning?	79	2	15
At your last IEP meeting was everybody there who provides services to your child?	46	NA	50
If not, were you given a written progress report before the meeting?	29	NA	34
Were you given a written progress report at the meeting?	70	NA	22

NA = not applicable.

Common themes may be found in responses to the open-ended questions. Table 4 lists sample responses grouped according to major themes. For the question, "What would make you feel more a partner in the decision-making process?," parents seemed mostly concerned about exchange of information (knowledge), procedures to be followed, and improved communication. In response to the question, "What has been a problem working with the people who serve your child?," responses seemed to reflect the categories of services, quality and attitudes of school personnel, and expectations of professionals regarding their children.

Discussion

The laws are in place requiring opportunities for parents to be fully informed and involved with their children's IEPs. Since P.L. 94–142 was enacted in 1975, parents have become more knowl-

Table 4 Sample Comments of Parents Pertaining to Open-ended Questions

Question: What would make you feel more a partner in the decision-making process?

Knowledge
- All parties being knowledgeable about the process of special education
- Role clarification—who is responsible for what?
- Schools should provide a list of appropriate contacts as a reference for parents
- Make sure parents are aware of other agencies that provide services for the child (i.e., rehab. services for the blind)

Procedures
- Obligation of school districts to show parents and give information about locating VI and O&M specialists/instructors
- IEPs: write objectives, criteria, goals, and how you will evaluate ongoing methods and timeliness
- Note to follow up on questions that were referred
- Teachers should be required to have contact with parents monthly

Communication
- Communicate concerns and questions to the appropriate people
- Leave detailed messages; give best times to call—both parents and school
- Communication notebooks
- Start high-level anxiety meetings with consensus building with what are two things that you can all agree on

Question: What has been a problem working with the people who serve your child?

Services and Quality of Personnel
- As she entered high school she was dropped and we were told she had all they had to offer.
- They feel that because he is developing, the need for specialized settings is less necessary. Also, we need a low vision exam to pinpoint his visual abilities.
- The vision teacher available is poorly qualified. There is only one teacher offered to us during the crucial preschool years.
- She is the first totally blind child the system has been made to serve.
- There is a lack of training in visual impairment.

Attitudes of School Personnel
- People are not accepting my child has normal intelligence.
- Small rural district, lack of choices, small prejudiced minds.
- I have a hard time disagreeing because I don't have a degree in ____.

Expectations
- Them thinking my kids are just like every other non-visually impaired kid, and expecting them to see small print or maps that they cannot see, or it strains their eyes.
- Their low educational expectations for my child in particular and the visually impaired population in general.

edgeable of those laws and involved with the education of their children. This study presents a "snapshot" of levels at which parents feel knowledgeable about and comfortable with the educational processes for their children. It demonstrates a continued need for professionals to provide information to and better communicate with parents thereby set in place procedures for ensuring true parent-professional partnerships. Further, the data suggests that parents also need to find additional ways of communicating with professionals and helping schools respond with appropriate and respectful approaches to providing education services to their children.

When three out of ten parents do not feel knowledgeable about their children's current abilities, when one in four are not comfortable attending IEP meetings, and four in ten parents do not feel knowledgeable about the services and programs available for their children, then professionals and parents must commit themselves to creating changes for the better.

The discrepancy between the percentage of parents who consider themselves to be involved in their children's education and the percentages regarding knowledge and comfort levels is noteworthy. Parents may not expect that professionals want them to fully participate. Consequently, they require less information and lower comfort levels to consider themselves involved. Although this is only conjecture, it behooves both professionals and parents to further explore why this discrepancy exists.

Another concern is that IEP meetings are being conducted without all personnel serving children in attendance. When this occurs, it is imperative that parents receive all written reports, along with interpretation of them, prior to the meeting. Each service provider's expertise and input are integral to the development of an appropriate individualized education program. Without this information, it is difficult for parents to offer input.

Yet another point of concern is the percentage of parents, 65 percent, who feel uncomfortable voicing disagreement with professionals' opinions regarding their children's progress and programming. When parents feel inadequate, ill informed, or lack confidence, their contributions will not be an equal part of the deliberations and decisions. Professionals and parents should have and express mutual respect for each others' opinions, leading to a productive partnership. Beginning steps to enhance this relationship may be the provision of more information, better communication, and established procedures designed for parents.

The difficulties expressed by parents must be taken seriously. Their voices should have a place in shaping the futures of educational services not only for their children but also for parents whose children have yet to receive a diagnosis, referral, assessment, or program in which to grow.

Based on our experience with NAPVI's national support and information network, we have found that motivated parents can go a long way toward solving difficult problems. With knowledge of special education laws, parents become more competent and qualified to offer substantial help for ensuring appropriate education for children. From the recommendations of parents responding to this survey, we see the wisdom that has come with experiences in providing for their children's edu-

cation. Families of children with visual impairment need more information and support in the following areas: legal rights, resources, educational programs and services available, educational needs of children with visual impairments, and planning for the future. Parent workshops, conferences, publications, and resource guides must be developed to address these areas. A strategic plan should be developed on how to reach parents with this information and support.

Lee Robinson, one of the founding parents of the NAPVI, states: "Parents must regard themselves as the long lasting resource and the only consistent persons who continually have their children's interest at heart throughout their lifetime. This organization now is a means to fulfill that function." Parent organizations are a valuable resource for encouraging and equipping parents with knowledge, confidence, and vision so they may take full advantage of their significant roles and positively affect their children's lives. NAPVI is dedicated to helping parents and professionals make the changes needed so that in the next Report to the Nation, parents reporting they feel knowledgeable about and comfortable with the education processes for their children will reach 100 percent.

Limitations of the Study

Parents who participated in this study either were members of a national organization for parents of visually impaired children or had attended events scheduled for such parents, indicating a level of direct involvement in the education of their children. Consequently, they may not represent all parents of children who have visual impairments, especially those for whom appropriate education services are not available.

References

National Association for Parents of the Visually Impaired. (1994, March). NAPVI Position Paper: Educational Reform. Watertown, MA: Author.

Crane, P., Cuthbertson, D., Ferrell, K. A., & Scherb, H. (1997). *Equals in partnership: Basic rights for families of children with visual impairment.* Watertown, MA: Hilton Perkins Program of the Perkins School for the Blind and the National Association for Parents of the Visually Impaired.

Goal 3

Universities, with a minimum of one full-time faculty member in the area of visual impairment, will prepare a sufficient number of educators of students with visual impairments to meet personnel needs throughout the country.

Submitted by Personnel Preparation, Division 17 Association for Education and Rehabilitation of the Blind and Visually Impaired
Prepared by Kay Alicyn Ferrell, Ph.D.

Background

Division 17 of AER has assumed responsibility for Goal 3. Volunteers were recruited and assigned to the tasks listed below. Other tasks will be identified as the National Agenda proceeds. Our efforts on Goal 3 have been somewhat hampered by the nature of academic schedules—faculty are either not available during the summer or are so busy running summer programs that time is sorely limited. But therein lies the problem that Goal 3 must address: a shortage of faculty in personnel preparation programs in education of students with visual impairments—too few people, stretched far too thin, preparing far too few graduates to meet the current (let alone the future) needs of students with visual impairments and multiple disabilities.

The current status of each of the national strategies for implementing Goal 3 follows.

1. *Develop a model of excellence for personnel preparation.* A Model Center of Excellence in Teacher Preparation was developed by Dr. Virginia Bishop and was reviewed by Dr. George Zimmerman. Drs. Tom Hehir and Louis Danielson of the Office of Special Education Programs (OSEP) were contacted regarding plans to offer regional, collaborative grants for personnel preparation. These contacts resulted in a policy forum sponsored by the National Association of State Directors of Special Education (NASDSE) convened on September 18–20, 1996. The proceedings of this meeting were published on January 21, 1997, and are available from NASDSE. Dr. Roseanne Silberman will announce publication of the NASDSE forum paper on the Internet.

2. *Encourage the establishment of a national research center on the education of students with visual impairments including those with multiple disabilities.* Dr. Sharon Sacks is in the process of determining the location and focus of current research centers (university, residential school, agency).

3. *Develop a collaborative national recruitment program in conjunction with the Association for Education and Rehabilitation of the Blind and Visually Impaired (AER).* Drs. Cay Holbrook and Marjorie Ward are determining the current status of AER recruitment efforts and will coordinate development of a plan for presentation to the AER Board of Directors, if necessary. The plan will also address retention efforts, recruitment at school district levels, and collaboration with the National Association of State Directors of Special Education (NASDSE) and Council of Administrators of Special Education of the Council for Exceptional Children (CASE/CEC).

4. *Encourage all university personnel preparation programs in the area of education of students with visual impairments to implement national standards.* The AER Board of Directors adopted Division 17's Standards for University Personnel Preparation Programs in Education of Students with Visual Impairments in October 1996. Division 17 has established a program review committee, chaired by Dr. Cay Holbrook, and programs should be able to submit their portfolios during the next year. Other members of the committee include Drs. Jane Erin, Toni Heinze, Alan Koenig, and George Zimmerman. Participants at the NASDSE forum suggested that federal grants be awarded only to programs that have received AER program approval.

Figure 1 identifies those states with teacher preparation programs. Stars indicate the programs within that state that appear likely to meet AER standards for teacher preparation programs.

5. *Determine the number of teachers of students with visual impairments as well as orientation and mobility specialists who graduated from university preparation programs in 1995.* Ensure that the number who will graduate in the year 2000 is the same or greater than the number for 1995. University programs were informally surveyed in 1994 and 1995 for the number of graduates. Problems within the questionnaire were such that a new survey was designed and reviewed by several university personnel in 1996 (see Table 1). This survey will be distributed annually until the year 2000 and should provide comparable year-to-year data. Results from the 1996 survey are contained in Figures 1 to 6. Note that a number of programs did not respond to the survey.

Respondents to the 1996 survey reported 960 students enrolled in personnel preparation programs during 1995–96, with 365 students graduating or otherwise completing programs (a "yield" of 38.0 percent—see Figure 2). Most of this yield were teachers of students with visual impairments [$n = 224$ (61.4 percent)—see Figure 3]. There were ninety-four new orientation and mobility specialists (25.8 percent of the yield); forty-three new dually certified teachers/O&M specialists (11.8 percent); one new teacher of students with deaf/blindness (.2 percent), and three new doctoral graduates (.8 percent). The number of bachelor's degrees awarded in visual impairment during 1995–96 remained about equal with Bowen and Klass's (1993) findings, while the number of master's degrees dropped 12.2 percent (see Figure 4).

Student enrollments and teacher yields, by state, are indicated in Figure 5. States with the highest populations (California, Michigan, Pennsylvania, and Texas) have the highest enrollments and graduates. The same data, reported by university programs, are found in Figure 6. Universities with enrollments in excess of forty students in 1995–96 are located in Arkansas, California, Colorado, Florida, Michigan, Nebraska, Pennsylvania, and Texas. States that produced more than twenty new teachers in 1995–96 were California, Florida, Illinois, Michigan, Pennsylvania, and Texas.

6. *Encourage collaborative planning among special education administrators and personnel preparation programs to establish and provide professional development programs.* Dr. Sandra Lewis has determined that four professional development agreements currently exist. The majority of programs utilize residential schools for student teaching and practicum experiences. Respondents rated the importance of close ties with a residential school to the preparation of quality teachers of blind and low vision students as a mean 5.9 on a seven-point scale (7 = essential, 4 = somewhat important, 1 = not important). A joint AER Division 17 and Council of Schools for the Blind task force to explore professional development partnerships has yet to be established.

7. *Develop, in conjunction with state departments of education, accurate counts of the number of students with visual impairments including those with multiple disabilities served in each state.* Drs. Gaylen Kapperman and Carol Love have contacted state consultants for students with visual impairments regarding their impressions of the accuracy of state counts. Sixty-four percent of the states reported that the annual count of children with visual impairments served under IDEA underestimated the actual number of children receiving services. A plan will be developed to obtain a more accurate count.

Utilizing federal estimates of the resident school-age population in 1993–94 (OSEP, 1995), a comparison was made between estimated prevalence rates for students with visual impairments and actual counts (see Figure 7). Jones and Collins (1966) estimated the prevalence of visual impairment in children at one-tenth of one percent, which would suggest that, nationally, there were 69,429 school-age children with visual impairment during the 1993–94 school year. More recent analyses (Nelson & Dimitrova, 1993; Wenger, Kaye, & LaPlante, 1996) have suggested the prevalence rate is closer to two-tenths of one percent, yielding 138,857 school-age students with visual impairments in 1993–94. Yet, the 1994 APH census registered only 53,576 individuals (APH, 1994), while the number of children served under IDEA during the same school year was only 24,892 (OSEP, 1995). These figures also illustrate the discrepancy between the APH census and the OSEP annual count, a gap that has been growing wider since 1978–79, when deaf/blind and multiply handicapped categories were introduced (see Figure 8).

8. *Establish systems of career leadership options that incorporate, among other categories, mentors, master*

Figure 1 University Programs in Blindness and Visual Impairments

(Source for Figures 1–8: Kay Alicyn Ferrell, University of Northern Colorado)

Table 1 Survey of College and University Programs 1995–96 School Year (9/1/95 through 8/31/96)

Program Category	Column 1		Column 2	Column 3	Column 4	Column 5	Column 6	Column 7	Column 8
	Total Number of Students Enrolled		Number of Students Exiting	Number Earning Bachelor's Degrees	Number Earning Master's Degrees	Number Eligible for Your State's Certification	Number Moving or Returning to Another State	Number Eligible for AER Certification	Number Leaving Program for Other Reasons
	Resident	Non-Resident							
Teacher of students with visual impairments (TSVI)									
Orientation & mobility specialist (O&M)									
Dual TSVI/O&M									
Teacher of students with deaf-blindness									
Doctoral program in special education/blind & visually impaired									

Notes for Columns 1–8:

1. Number of resident and non-resident students enrolled in each of the five program categories leading to degree and/or certification between 9/1/95 and 8/31/96. Include academic, year, summer, and extension or distance education formats. DO NOT include individuals enrolled in courses who are *not* pursuing a degree and/or certification program. Count a student only once in each cell, either as TSVI, O&M, Dual, Deaf-blind, or Doctoral.

Complete columns 2 through 8 for each individual student according to how you initially classified that student in Column 1.

2. Number of students in each of the five program categories who completed their preparation for a degre and/or certification between 9/1/95 and 8/31/96 who are exiting the university. These students will NOT be enrolled after 9/1/96.

If an individual completed requirements for one type of program in 1995–96, such as TSVI, and decided to continue at the college/university to add on O&M, INCLUDE them here, *if they are employed in the field.*

For doctoral students, count them in Column 2 IF THEY HAVE COMPLETED ALL REQUIREMENTS FOR THEIR DOCTORAL DEGREE (up to and including defense of the dissertation), even if the degree has not actually been awarded.

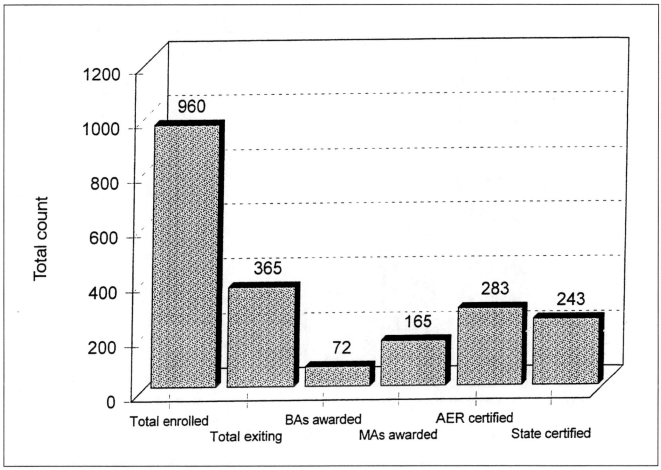

Source: Goal 3, The National Agenda

Figure 2 Students Enrolled and Exiting 1995–96

3. Number of students in each of the five program categories who completed all requirements for a bachelor's degree between 9/1/95 and 8/31/96. Include those individuals who may have completed their requirements during this time period but whose degree will not actually be awarded until later.

4. Number of students in each of the five program categories who completed all requirements for a master's degree between 9/1/95 and 8/31/96. Include those individuals who may have completed their requirements during this time period, but whose degree will not actually be awarded until later.

5. Number of students in each program category who became eligible for YOUR STATE's certification/endorsement/licensure between 9/1/95 and 8/31/96. DO NOT include individuals who became eligible for temporary or emergency certificates; the key concept here is identification of the number of individuals who achieved your state's full certification/endorsement/licensure.

6. Number of students in each program category who exited the program between 9/1/95 and 8/31/96 and who, TO THE BEST OF YOUR KNOWLEDGE, intended to move or return to ANOTHER STATE.

7. Number of students eligible for certification from AER, either as a teacher or as an O&M specialist, between 9/1/95 and 8/31/96, regardless of whether the person actually applies.

8. If there were other individuals enrolled in your program between 9/1/95 and 8/31/96 who left the program for some other reason, include them here.

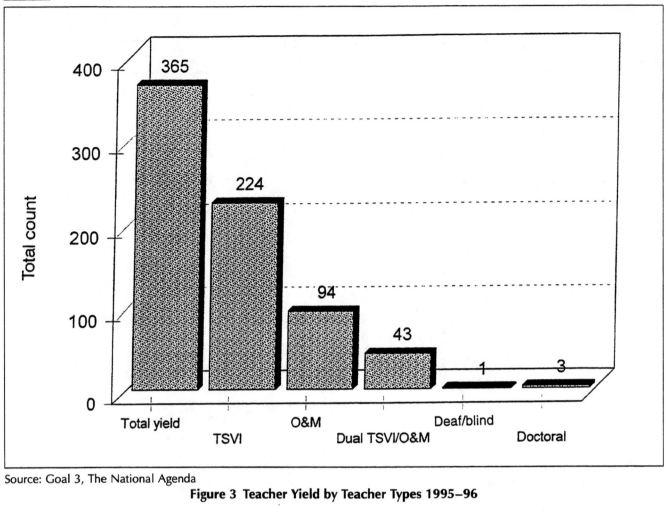

Source: Goal 3, The National Agenda

Figure 3 Teacher Yield by Teacher Types 1995–96

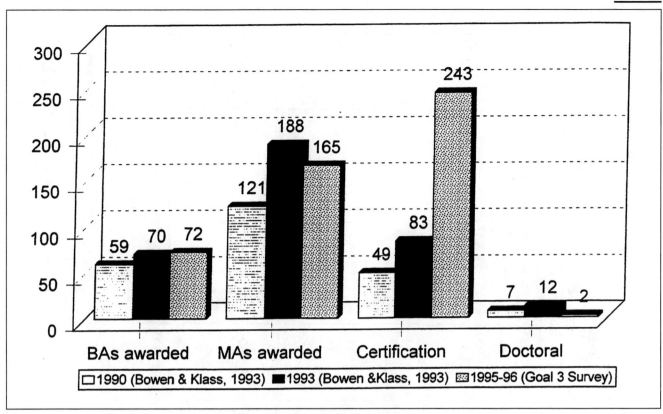

Source: Goal 3, The National Agenda. Note that Goal 3 Survey data (1995–96) are not exactly comparable to Bowen & Klass, due to differences in methods of data collection.

Figure 4 Comparison of Graduates [Bowen & Klass (1993); Goal 3 Survey]

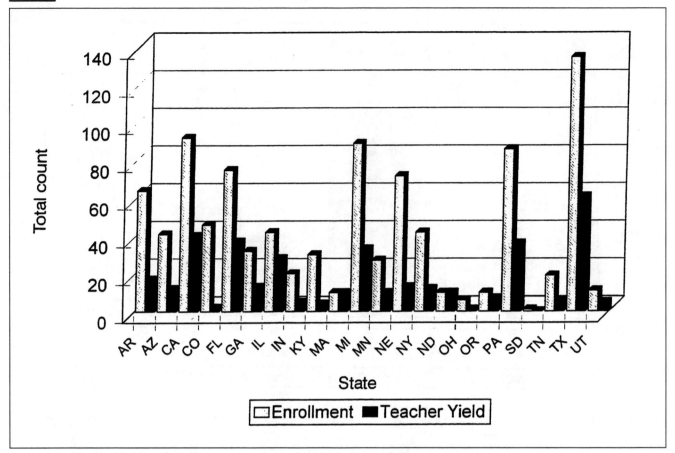

Source: Goal 3, The National Agenda

Figure 5 Student Enrollments vs. Teacher Yields, 1995–96 (by state)

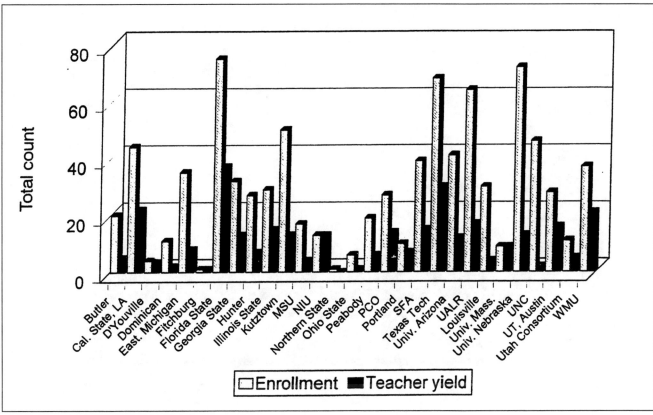

Source: Goal 3, The National Agenda

Figure 6 Student Enrollments vs. Teacher Yields, 1995–96 (by college or university)

teachers, master orientation and mobility (O&M) specialists, and teachers-as-researchers. This strategy is being explored with AER certification committees to revise categories for recognizing leadership activities.

9. *Facilitate a means for achieving reciprocity of teacher credentialing among all states.* Dr. Sandra Lewis is completing a study of current credentialing/licensing regulations in each state.

10. *Identify incentives by which school districts can be encouraged to ensure that teachers with "emergency credentials" become appropriately credentialed in the area of education for students with visual impairments including those with multiple disabilities.* This strategy has yet to be implemented.

Implications of Findings

The greatest difficulty confronting the implementation of Goal 3 is the inaccurate count of students with visual impairments and the resulting inability to plan for the future. Without accurate counts, we will never know if we have achieved our goal of preparing enough teachers. Greater efforts must be made to document how students are served, rather than how they are labeled. The U.S. Department of Education has now recognized the issues facing personnel preparation in blindness and visual impairment and has taken steps to assist the field in planning collaboratively for the future. The success of these efforts remains to be seen.

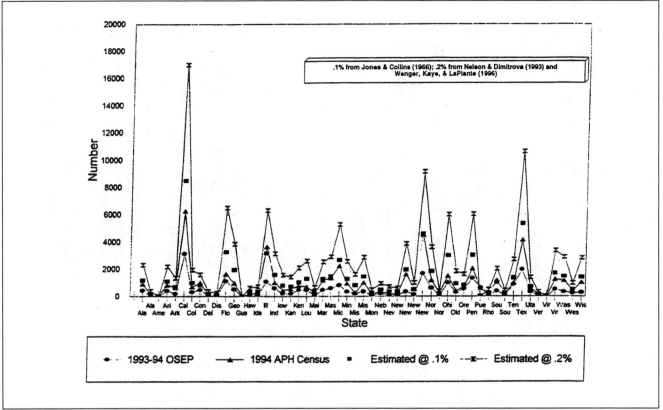

Figure 7 Children with Visual Impairments (Annual counts vs. prevalence rates)

Recommendations for Further Research

We recommend, and will implement, ongoing data collection efforts to track the numbers of new teachers produced annually. Additional research is needed on:

1. The numbers and types of teachers who leave the field, and why.
2. The number of children with multiple disabilities who are being served by teachers of students with visual impairments and/or orientation and mobility specialists.

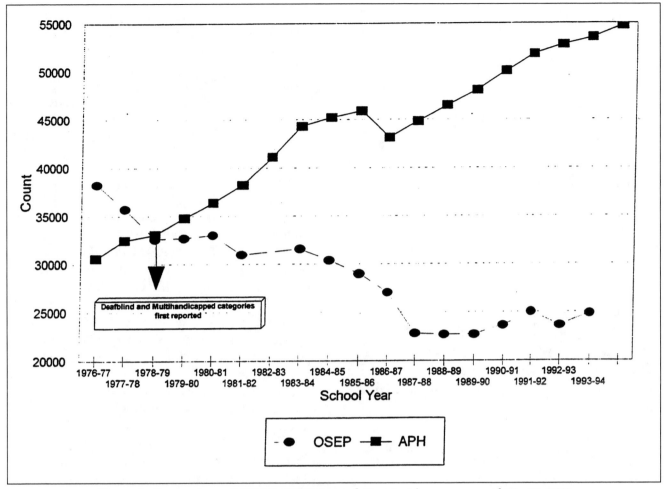

Figure 8 Comparison of APH & OSEP Annual Counts (since passage of P.L. 94-142)

References

American Printing House for the Blind (APH). (1994). *Distribution of federal quota based on the January 3, 1994 registration of eligible students.* Louisville, KY: Department of Educational and Advisory Services, American Printing House for the Blind.

Bowen, M. L., & Klass, P. H. (1993). Low-incidence special education teacher preparation: A supply and capacity pilot study. *Teacher Education and Special Education, 16,* 248–256.

Jones, J. W., & Collins, A. P. (1966). *Educational programs for visually handicapped children.* Washington, DC: U. S. Government Printing Office.

Nelson, K. A., & Dimitrova, G. (1993). Severe visual impairment in the United States and in each state, 1990. *Journal of Visual Impairment & Blindness,* 80–85.

Office of Special Education Programs (OSEP). (1995). *Seventeenth annual report to Congress on the implementation of the individuals with disabilities education act.* Washington, DC: U. S. Department of Education.

Wenger, B. L., Kaye, H. S., & LaPlante, M. P. (1996). *Disabilities statistics abstract No. 15: Disabilities among children.* Washington, DC: U. S. Department of Education, National Institute on Disability and Rehabilitation Research (NIDRR).

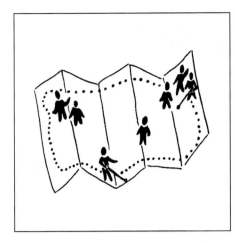

Goal 4

Service providers will determine caseloads based on the needs of students and will require ongoing professional development for all teachers and orientation and mobility instructors.

Submitted by the Association of State Educational Consultants for the Visually Impaired (ASECVI) Prepared by Sharon Knoth

The National Outlook

In October 1995, the Association of State Educational Consultants for the Visually Impaired (ASECVI) surveyed state departments of education and residential schools for the blind and visually impaired. The purpose was to gather information on how these entities determine caseloads based on the individual needs of students who are blind or visually impaired. Forty-seven states responded to a survey (94 percent) that consisted of a telephone inquiry or paper flyer asking:

1. Do your state regulations dictate specific numbers/ranges for class size?
2. Do your state regulations dictate specific numbers/ranges for caseloads?
3. Do these regulations differ by exceptionality area or disability category or are they uniform throughout the various exceptionalities?
4. Does your state have (or is in the process of developing) guidelines or procedures for deter-

mining caseloads and/or class sizes? If so, may we have a copy?
5. If so, are these guidelines specific to the area of blindness and visual impairment or are they applicable to all exceptionalities?
6. If your state has guidelines or procedures for the area of blindness and visual impairment, do they differentiate between itinerant versus resource versus residential programs, etc.?*

Of the forty-seven states that responded, 72 percent had either regulatory standards or policy guidelines for the determination of class sizes and caseloads in special education programs.† Fifty-seven percent of the states responding had regulatory standards or policy guidelines that were specific to blindness and visual impairment. Of the 55 percent of states responding whose regulatory standards contained language with numerical limits on class sizes or caseloads, 81 percent spoke specifically to our segment of the population. Two states stipulated ratios of staff to students in lieu of specific numerical caseload limits and two states utilized both numerical limits and a ratio of staff to students. See Table 1 for details.

The premise of the Individuals with Disabilities Education Act (IDEA) is encompassed in its first word—"individuals." As ASECVI worked on this segment of Goal 4 and surveyed what various states have in place (and what the individual schools within that state utilize) concerning caseload development, there were numerous discussions among our membership. Each state is unique and our organization believed that *we must not lose sight of the fact that each student within each school district and region of our country has divergent and varied needs.* Through these discussions it became apparent that there simply is not one best manner by which states should determine caseloads for students who are blind or visually impaired. Let us take an in-depth look at what some of our colleagues are using to ensure that caseloads are based on the individual needs of blind and visually impaired students.

Unique Qualities of Regulatory Standards

Vignette 1

Jenna is a veteran teacher of students who are blind and visually impaired and works in a rural area.

Table 1 State Response to the ASECVI Survey

Class Size/Caseload Regulation/Guidelines Information	Numerical Reference for Class Size or Caseload	No Numerical Reference
Regulations—Nonspecific to the visually impaired	Idaho, Massachusetts, New Nexico	Indiana
Regulations—specific to the visually impaired	Alabama, Illinois, Iowa, Kansas, Kentucky, Louisiana, Michigan, Nebraska, Nevada, New Jersey, North Carolina, Ohio, Utah, West Virginia, Wisconsin	
Guidelines—nonspecific to the visually impaired	Oklahoma, Tennessee	South Dakota
Guidelines—specific to the visually impaired	Arizona, California, Delaware, Georgia, Missouri, Oregon	Arkansas (ration listed), Colorado, North Dakota, South Carolina, (rations listed), Texas, Virginia
No guidelines or regulations	Connecticut, Florida, Hawaii, Maine, Maryland, Minnesota, Mississippi, New Hampshire, New York, Rhode Island, Vermont, Washington, Wyoming	

Currently she has a Resource Room at an elementary school located twenty-five miles from her office. Three students are enrolled, one of whom is a braille reader. One student, enrolled in the multi-handicapped program, spends the first two hours of the day at this school. The braille reader is just mastering braille and has difficulties with some assignments. There is no paraprofessional with knowledge of braille at the school. Before Jenna leaves for the day, she goes through this student's assignments and circles or prints any short form words that may prove difficult for the student.

Two days a week, she spends the remainder of her time at a junior high school located twenty

*Table 1 is a brief analysis of the states that responded to the survey. Nowhere in this report have the actual class size numbers or caseload ranges utilized by a particular state been restated. Because of state-specific regulations, the data collected and being referenced herein are not transferable from state to state. The reader is encouraged to contact a specific state and request a copy of their guidelines or regulations for more specific information.

†Two states have regulatory guidelines for general education that were inferred to cover special education programs as well.

miles from the elementary school. It too is in a rural area and takes her thirty minutes to travel the distance. At the junior high school she has five students, two of whom are braille readers. One of these is experiencing difficulties keeping up with his course work due to the volume of reading materials and the lack of their availability in braille. Jenna is teaching braille to a volunteer so she can transcribe materials and she often uses her own time for transcribing materials.

Twice each week Jenna splits afternoons between two high schools, forty-five minutes apart in the district. She has two low vision students at one high school and one braille reader at the other. All three are precollege students. Jenna has a volunteer in the community, a braille reader, who assists the braillist. Jenna works with all three students on transitional activities and independent living skills. Many days she works with students after school and then drives them home. There is no instructor to provide needed O&M services during the school year. However, two students attended a summer outreach program at a special school and received O&M instruction.

Fridays, Jenna's time is spent evaluating new "potential" students, visiting her "consultation caseload," and performing other professional duties.

She provides three in-service training programs annually. Her day generally starts at her office and can require travel to any one of eighteen sites within the special education planning district. She travels an average of eight hundred miles a month and puts in many hours of noncompensated overtime. At any given period she may be involved in a multidisciplinary team assessment of several students. She worries about the additional load of an added student.

Jenna struggles with the need to provide appropriate services for the students she is already working with and the requirement to offer services in students' home schools whenever possible. Her supervisor has been seeking a part-time teacher of students with visual impairments to assist her since budgetary constraints do not permit hiring a full-time teacher. To date he has been unable to locate anyone. Nonetheless, the special education director is not concerned because state regulations permit Jenna a caseload of fourteen students, excluding consultations. They are well within the law.

Discussion

This vignette typifies a rural caseload for a teacher of students with visual impairments. It is common for a rural district to have only one such teacher or even share a teacher with another district. This results in the teacher assuming a variety of roles, many of which are unique to the area of blindness and visual impairments. Rarely would you find other teachers serving as a member of the multidisciplinary assessment team, the sole consultant in a given exceptionality area for the district, the primary overseer for that disability's resource room, and the one responsible for providing in-service or awareness training for the community. Furthermore, although some state regulations take into consideration the number of braille readers in the caseload, none specifically address the role the teacher of students with visual impairments plays on the multidisciplinary assessment/triennial assessment team. For some communities, this role can consume a vast amount of time.

Of the states that sent us a copy of their regulations, only one had regulations addressing curriculum for O&M, communication, personal adjustment skills, and vocational education. This is not to say that other states do not have curricula for these areas. If a school district is planning on developing procedures for determining caseloads, it may wish to explore various curricula used specifically for blind and visually impaired students if their district does not have one. Another idea would be to develop local descriptions of various courses taught or offered in the program for students with visual impairments. This may provide some insight about time allocations for various skill areas (see Goal 8—Core Curriculum).

Vignette 2

Warren is the supervisor of the program for students with visual impairments for a metropolitan special education planning district. He has two full- and one half-time teachers of students with visual impairments and one O&M instructor in the program. These teachers serve forty-three students aged three through twenty. The geographical area covered by the planning district is fifty-five square miles. Warren also supervises the related services personnel and the program for students with hearing impairments, serves as case conference coordinator, and chairs case conferences. There are a total of twelve elementary, nine middle, and three high schools in the district.

The preschool program receives consultation services from a teacher of students with visual impairments for six students, two of whom have multiple impairments. Mary, the O&M instructor, consults on a bimonthly basis with the preschool program. Recently, Warren has contracted "after hours" for her to begin working directly with one of the students on pre-cane skills. Mary has agreed to come into work thirty minutes early two days per month on a contractual basis to provide these services, but is hesitant to take any more time than that "away from her own family." Mary works on a regular basis with twenty-three students throughout the program for the visually impaired.

One full-time teacher of students with visual impairments, Harriet, has been with the district fifteen years; the other, Melanee, is new. Based out of a centrally located school, Harriet works with twelve elementary-level students, four of whom are braille readers. A full-time paraprofessional and braille transcriber are available to assist her. Two of the braille readers are beginning braille readers. Harriet has requested the assistance of another licensed teacher of students with visual impairments. She believes that without that assistance, she will be unable to teach efficient braille skills to her students. She sends weekly memos to Warren that specifically state her concerns with the elementary program. However, Warren has been informed that no additional elementary classroom space is available for an additional resource room.

Last year, Warren found Stella, a teacher of students with learning disabilities who was willing to take the coursework necessary for a visually impaired endorsement. State certification standards permit him to hire a noncertified teacher on what is called a "Limited License" or "Emergency Credential" when he is unable to hire a fully qualified teacher. Warren has applied for limited visually impaired licensure for Stella, who has taken the introductory braille and physiology and anatomy of the eye courses. Warren uses her on a part-time basis to assist students whose case conferences have placed them in buildings other than where the elementary visually impaired program is located. At this time, Stella has nine visually impaired students in her caseload, one of whom is a braille reader. She travels to five elementary schools within the district, a different one each morning of the week.

Melanee graduated last year from a university teachers of students with visual impairments training program, is full of innovative ideas, and is very interested in assessing the functional vision of her students. Although Warren sees the advantages of this, he knows there are not enough hours in the day for him to permit her to spend time on items not required by state/federal regulations or local guidelines. They have a "working agreement" that enables her to conduct functional vision assessments once her other assignments are complete. She is currently working on local procedures that would infuse functional vision assessments into various components of the visually impaired program.

Melanee has six middle school students and ten high school students in her caseload, all of whom are seen one or two days a week for approximately thirty to forty minutes on a consultant basis. Exceptions are two braille readers at the high school whom she sees daily for forty-five minutes. The paraprofessional is in this building all day and the students or their general education teachers "sign up" for her time. When she is not working directly with one of the students, she is assisting in ordering and preparing materials for all the students in Melanee's caseload. The remainder of Melanee's time is spent assessing potential students for the visually impaired program and assisting with student evaluations. She wishes she had fewer students and more time to devote to functional vision assessments.

Warren knows that in the past year, five special education and seven general education teachers have been laid off because of budget cuts, and the district is moving toward more inclusive programming for special needs pupils. He seriously doubts that the school board will permit hiring another teacher of children with visual impairments. This is especially true considering that the state guidelines have caseload recommendations well within the range of the programs he supervises. Nonetheless, he is trying to provide more time for all the paraprofessionals of the visually impaired to receive intensive training and is attempting to maneuver schedules to allow Stella to take on more visually impaired program responsibilities.

Discussion

This vignette is an example of a fairly typical urban visually impaired program. Generally speaking, a continuum of services exists, but so too does the need for additional staff. Far too often budgetary constraints, transient populations, and lack of adequate space for classes are stumbling blocks for the advancement of all programs—not just special education. Unless guidelines look at the visually impaired program as a whole, take into consideration the specific needs of the students enrolled in the program and the program's potential growth, contemplate the various roles the teacher of students with visual impairments will fulfill, envision the "fit" into general education's goals and long-range plans, and have administrative support, the potential for long-term influence is inhibited.

Unique Qualities of Policy Guidelines

The majority of the guidelines reviewed by ASECVI referenced the need to account for the severity/intensity of student needs; consulting with medical personnel, families, and community resources; travel time; securing and preparing specialized materials and equipment; record keeping; and utilization of paraprofessionals. Several guidelines spoke to the need for involving the teacher of students with visual impairments as well as the local administrator when setting up caseloads. All of this is consistent with the Carnegie Corporation Report's (1996) reference to school-based decision making. Self-evaluation components and rating scales are a prevalent means by which many state guidelines review and determine caseloads for blind and visually impaired programs. Let's look at what might be a good foundation on which a particular school district may begin planning for comprehensive guidelines for caseloads for such programs.

Strategies for School-Based Decisions

The booklet *Print and Braille Literacy—Selecting Appropriate Learning Media* (Spungin, 1990) states that "successful performance of the visually impaired student in the classroom and in other educational settings rests with both the parents and the professional"—a theme we see repeated throughout this *Report to the Nation*. Any discussion on how schools may examine the procedures utilized for determining caseloads must include parents, teachers, and the administration—basically the school community. School-based decisions have the benefit of knowing the individual community's needs and deficits as well as the resources available. This insight is invaluable and not available at the state or regional level, which is the probable impetus for the majority of state regulations as well as guidelines referencing local decisions.

School-based decision making is a means of imparting ownership to all involved. Many schools have already moved toward this process with their general education programs. Frequently, low-incidence areas are omitted. This omission is more attributable to the fact that the leader of the visually impaired program (typically the teacher of students with visual impairments) is often not a full-time member of the school's faculty and therefore not considered or available for the planning process. If the visually impaired program decides to develop guidelines for caseload determinations, it is beneficial to build on whatever school-based decision platform already exists. Here are some questions the school-based decision-making team may want to review.

- Where does the visually impaired program currently stand in relation to the overall school system?
- Does the school have a strategic planning team currently in place?
- Is the program for students with visual impairments a part of that team?
- Was the visually impaired program a part of the school's long-range planning process?
- Is there an up-to-date listing of all personnel involved in the visually impaired program?
- Is there an up-to-date listing of students receiving services from the visually impaired program (including those receiving consultative services)?

- What about students who are not considered eligible, yet the visually impaired program consults with their teachers from time to time?
- Is the visually impaired program represented in any building-based student assistant team?
- What are the current procedures utilized for determining caseloads within the visually impaired program?
- Are they specified in writing or are they generalities?
- Does the visually impaired program conduct in-service sessions or workshops during the year? If so, how frequently and with whom?
- What are the current procedures for determining class sizes in our building/district?
- Are they applicable for the visually impaired program?
  If not, can they be modified to be applicable?
- Are there measurable and defendable reasons why we believe the visually impaired program should not use these same procedures?
- Does our VI program currently have a specified curriculum that it implements?
  If so, does it cover the following core curriculum requisites for blind and visually impaired learners: braille, use of low vision, orientation and mobility, personal adjustment training, daily living skills, transition training and communication skills?
  If no interventions occur at this time, what do we envision our visually impaired program will look like in five years?
  Is this a realistic goal?
  What will it take for us to get to that point?
  Do we have the necessary human resources to achieve this goal?
- What additional resources might assist us in achieving this goal?
  How will we know when the visually impaired program is "there"?
- Does our visually impaired program follow its graduates to ensure that we are providing students with the skills necessary to be literate adults in our community?
- Do we know what percentage of our graduates enter gainful employment after exiting the visually impaired program?
- Do we know what percentage of our graduates go on for further education after exiting the visually impaired program?

As school-based decision teams work collaboratively, disagreements will inevitably occur—it is only human nature. This is why it is important for all members who have a stake in the outcome of the process to be involved from the start. Honest, open discussions need to address disagreements with the true spirit of teamwork. Creative problem solving and nominal group processes for consensus building are means the team may choose to explore. Change does not come without some strife.

The Intrinsic Principles of Caseload Management

A brief overview of the data ASECVI gathered reinforces the need for flexibility and local control over decisions regarding caseloads for low-incidence areas such as blindness and visual impairment. The California Department of Education's *Program Guidelines for Visually Impaired Individuals* (1986) has an excellent definition that is applicable to this document and our discussions:

> The guidelines have been developed as a resource for parents, staff, and administrators in assessing, identifying, planning, providing, evaluating, and improving the quality and cost effectiveness of programs serving visually impaired students.

The development of any guidelines must involve all key associates from the very beginning. The following is an overview of guidelines we have reviewed that were selected because of their unique quantities or difference from other state guidelines; no inference of commendation or superiority is intended. The states are mentioned by name as a courtesy and out of respect for their labors.

The California Guidelines (1986) list the following elements:
Developing a process for establishing and monitoring the class size or a caseload of the teacher of students with visual impairments or orientation and mobility specialist, based on the time required for:

- Providing instruction based on the severity or intensity of students' needs.
- Consulting with the classroom teacher and other staff, including consultation when the student is not receiving direct instruction.
- Consulting and assisting parents.
- Traveling necessary to carry out responsibilities.
- Securing and preparing needed specialized materials, media, and equipment.
- Attending meetings, preparing reports, and rec-

ord keeping. Include in the process ongoing communication between the staff member and the responsible supervisor or administrator to ensure that students are receiving appropriate instruction and services in accordance with the IEP and the changing needs of students. Establish local caseloads and class sizes based on the age and severity of the need of the students being served and the instruction and services needed to meet these needs.

Colorado is another state with a unique perspective on caseload management. Through a team study that has been in process for several years, a three-pronged approach to caseload management has been developed.

1. Direct and indirect services to students (severity of needs determiners).
2. Related professional responsibilities (parent contact, supervision of support staff, referral assignments, writing reports, in-service responsibilities, consultation, materials preparation, ordering and inventorying materials).
3. Travel time.

The North Dakota Department of Education offers yet another means for looking at caseload development. The focus of their guidelines is on student-specific needs and intensity of services. They use a rating scale that is part of the IEP process. As the case conference committee reviews the assessment data and discusses student-specific strengths and needs, the student is rated from 0–4 in the following areas:

Medical
Reading medium
Compensatory skill needs
Environmental and instructional adjustments

The "starting point" for determining the intensity of services a student needs is based on his or her total score, with the case conference committee having the discretion to decide on the actual services the student receives.

Our final review comes from Texas. A grant from the Texas Education Agency to the Texas School for the Blind and Visually Impaired produced a comprehensive training guide entitled *A Guide to Quality Programs for Students with Visual Impairments* (1990). The *Guide* has a process generally anticipated to take a district three years from beginning to end. A brief outline of that process includes:

Phase One: A self-study of key program components (accurate listing of students enrolled in program, discussion of issues regarding the student's eligibility enrolled in program, amount and type of services the student receives, roles and responsibilities of staff members, service delivery options, etc.)

Phase Two: A process wherein the district is able to document the program's strengths and deficits.

Phase Three: A proactive phase wherein the district fosters program growth and development while meeting the changing needs of the students enrolled.

Several of the guidelines reviewed used one or more of those listed above and added specificity for compliance with particular local and state regulations. As stated earlier, there is no one "best way" for a particular state or school district to determine caseloads for visually impaired students. What is evident is that no matter which method is used, whether guidelines or regulations, there is always room for individualization and flexibility. Those states with regulatory language had a means by which a district could justifiably seek a waiver or extension of the numerical or linguistic limits imposed.

Those states that had guidelines allowed for flexibility and individualization to meet each district's unique needs. Special education is ever changing; and, as we evolve with it, our profession needs to ensure that our student's vision-specific needs are fully addressed. We can attempt to provide guidance, but ultimately how each school district goes about doing this must be left in their hands.

References

Carnegie Corporation. (1996). *Years of promise: A comprehensive learning strategy for America's children.* New York: Carnegie Corporation.

Caton, H. (Ed.). (1991). *Print and braille literacy— Selecting appropriate learning media.* Louisville, KY: American Printing House for the Blind.

Hazekamp, J. & Lundin, J. (Eds.). (1986). *Program guidelines for visually impaired individuals.* Sacramento: California Department of Education.

National Education Goals Panel. (1996). *National education goals report: Building a nation of learners.* Washington, DC: U. S. Government Printing Office.

Spungin, S. J. (1990). *Braille literacy: Issues for blind persons, families, professionals, and producers of braille.* New York: American Foundation for the Blind.

Toelle, N. M. (1990). *Guide to quality programs for students with visual impairments (A).* Austin: Texas Education Agency/Texas School for the Blind and Visually Impaired.

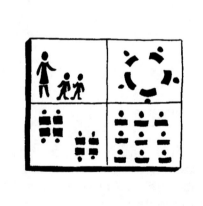

Goal 5

Local education programs will ensure that all students have access to a full array of placement options.

Submitted by Council of Schools for the Blind (COSB)
Prepared by Eugene McMahon, Ed.D., The New York Institute for Special Education

Information About Placements Given by IEP Teams to Parents of Children with Visual Impairments

The Individuals with Disabilities Education Act (IDEA) requires Local Education Agencies (LEAs) to provide all disabled children with a free and appropriate education. The U.S. Office of Education clarified the requirements of this law for children with visual impairments in a policy paper issued in 1995. The Policy Guidance Memorandum (Heuman, 1996) acknowledges that in order to provide all children with visual impairments a free and appropriate education, an array of placement options is needed. Goal 5 of the National Agenda deals with the availability of this array of placements (Corn, Hatlen, Huebner, Ryan, & Siller, 1995). The goal states that LEAs will ensure that all students have access to a full array of placement options. Determination of what constitutes an appropriate educational placement for a particular child is the responsibility of a multidisciplinary team. This team, formed by the LEA, includes and receives input from the child's parents. Parental input received great emphasis in the 1997 reauthorization of the IDEA.

It would be a difficult or impossible task to directly measure the appropriateness of educational placements for visually impaired children to determine if the full array of placement options is, in fact, available. As such, an indirect approach is employed. To have access to a full array of placement options, parents, as parties knowledgeable about the needs of their child, must be informed that these choices exist.

Referring to parents of children with learning disabilities, Brantlinger (1987) states:

> When parents have less than complete information, viable choices are not likely and special education professionals may simply be facilitating the agenda of those who wish to educate only certain learners in mainstream settings. (p. 110)

This statement applies equally to parents of visually impaired children and to all situations in which school-district decision makers have preset biases toward any type of placement. The purpose of the current study is to determine what information about placements is given to parents of children with visual impairments by their IEP teams.

Procedure

A survey instrument was developed in which parents of visually impaired children were asked to state whether they were given information at their IEP meeting only about the placement being recommended for their child or whether other placement options were also explained to them. For purposes of the survey, "explained" was defined in the following way:

> In order to be marked as explained/discussed, the option must have been explained in detail and be specific to the school district. For example, the IEP team would say, "Johnny could be in a mainstreamed class at Elmont Elementary School and receive itinerant services for the visually impaired in the resource room of that school," if these were the services he needed. Another example would be that Johnny could attend the state residential school for the blind, if these were the services he needed.

If parents said that other options had been explained, they were asked to check off which options they were. The options listed were those used by the U.S. Department of Education when collecting data on placement pursuant to IDEA (Westat, 1997). Students placed in correctional facilities were left off the list.

Regular Classroom—Children and youths who receive the majority of their education program in regular classes. May receive special education outside the regular classroom for no more than 21 percent of the school day.

Resource Room—Children and youths who receive education programs in the resource room. May receive special education outside the regular classroom for at least 21 percent but no more than 60 percent of the school day.

Separate Class—Children and youths who receive education programs in separate classes outside the regular classroom for more than 69 percent of the school day. (This does not include pupils in separate day or residential public and private schools.)

Public Separate School Facility—Children and youths who receive services in a public separate day school for greater than 50 percent of their school day.

Private Separate School Facility—Children and youths who receive services in a private separate day school at public expense for greater than 50 percent of their school day.

Public Residential Facility—Children and youths who receive services in a public residential school for greater than 50 percent of their school day.

Private Residential Facility—Children and youths who receive services in a private residential school at public expense for greater than 50 percent of their school day.

Homebound/Hospital Placement—Children and youths who receive services in a homebound/hospital placement.

Subjects for the survey were obtained from three sources:

1. The membership roster of the National Association for Parents of the Visually Impaired.
2. Lists obtained through State Vision Consultants.
3. Parents of children attending member schools of the Council of Schools for the Blind (COSB).

A total of 1,525 surveys were distributed. Of these, 406 were returned. Forty-seven of the returned surveys were not completed. The majority of these surveys had notes indicating that their children were no longer of school age. A total of 359 completed surveys were returned. After eliminating the returned blank surveys, a completion rate of 24.3 percent was obtained.

Information about a number of demographic variables was collected on the survey. One of those variables was the current placement of their visually impaired child. Table 1 shows the current placement of the children of survey respondents. Eighty-nine surveys did not indicate current placement. The last column in the table reports comparison data from the *Nineteenth Annual Report to Congress* (U.S. Department of Education, 1997).

The table shows that 72.6 percent of the placements are in public school buildings with 53.7 percent in regular class, 6.3 percent in resource room, and 12.6 percent in separate classes in public school. Placements in the category of separate day school accounted for 6.7 percent of the sample, while residential placements equaled 19.3 percent. In comparison, the data from the Report to Congress shows that 84.24 percent of the placements are in public school buildings, 4.79 percent are in separate schools, and 10.44 percent are in residential placements. Compared to the Report to Congress, this survey sample has a smaller percentage of students in public schools and a larger percentage in separate day and residential schools. The skewing of the sample for the study is likely a result of the oversampling of parents in COSB schools.

Results

The first research question was whether parents report that their IEP team gives them information about only the recommended placement or whether they receive information about various placement options. Table 2 shows how parents responded to this question.

Over 70 percent of the 359 parents reported that they were only given information about the placement the IEP team recommended for their child. When a parent indicated that multiple placement options were explained, they were asked to indicate which options were explained. They chose from the menu of eight placement options described above. Table 3 shows the variability in the number of placement options that were explained; this information is presented graphically in Figure 1.

The table shows that for the 30 percent of the parents who received information on more than the recommended placement, 48.7 percent received information on only two options. Thirty percent received information on three options. The frequency of number of explained options continues to drop across the range, with only one respondent (1.3 percent) reporting that all eight options were explained.

Table 4 presents data on the frequency of placement options that are explained when multiple options are described.

Regular class placement is explained 28.0 percent of the time when multiple options are explained. Similarly, resource room is explained in 19.6 percent of the cases and separate class in public school is explained in 13.3 percent of the cases.

Table 1 Current Placement of Visually Impaired Children

	Survey Demographics		Demographics of the 19th Report to Congress
	Frequency	**Percent**	**Percent**
Regular class	145	53.7	45.94
Resource room	17	6.3	21.09
Separate class	34	12.6	17.21
Public separate school	8	3.0	2.9
Private separate school	10	3.7	1.89
Public residential	34	12.6	9.51
Private residential	18	6.7	.93
Homebound/hospital	4	1.5	.53
Total	270	100.0	100.0

Table 2 Information about Placement Options Given to Parents by IEP Teams

	Frequency	Percent
Various options	101	28.1
Recommended option only	258	71.9
Total	359	100.0

Table 3 Number of Placement Options Explained to Parents Who Received Information on More Than the Recommended Option

Number	Frequency	Percent
2	37	48.7
3	23	30.3
4	8	10.5
5	5	6.6
7	2	2.6
8	1	1.3
Total	76	100.0

Table 4 Options Explained When Multiple Options Are Explained

Placement	Frequency	Percent
Regular class	63	28.0
Resource room	44	19.6
Separate class	30	13.3
Public special day school	25	11.1
Private special day school	15	6.7
Public residential	31	13.8
Private residential	12	5.3
Homebound	5	2.2
Total	225	100.0

Special day school is explained in 17.8 percent of the cases and residential placement is included in 19.2 percent of the cases. Over 60 percent of the time, a special placement (public, private, day, or residential) is not explained to parents. Likewise, over 40 percent of the time, parents are not given explanations of placement within public school.

Discussion

Despite the rhetoric regarding the need for parent input in IEP decision making, the results of this

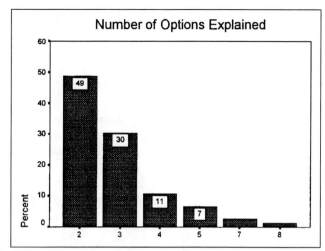

Figure 1 Number of Placement Options Explained to Parents Who Received Information on More Than the Recommended Option

study suggest that parents are not given the information they need to truly participate. In 70 percent of the cases, the amount of information given to them involves only the placement option that the district is recommending. In half of the remaining 30 percent, when multiple options were explained, the districts explained only two options rather than the full continuum.

The definition of the term "explained" used in this study necessitates a higher level of information than is typically thought of as required by school districts. To achieve the role parents should have in the decision-making process that was envisioned when IDEA was originally passed, and expanded in the recently completed reauthorization, parents need more than information sheets or pamphlets describing general options. In a study of parents of children with learning disabilities, Brantlinger (1987) found that:

> Parents seemed generally unaware of the cascade of services that might be available to their children. Many, however, did remember that they had received a booklet for parents at a case conference. Some claimed that they had read it, but they knew no more about the procedural and integration concepts than those who claimed never to have received a copy (p. 98).

Parents must be informed about how their child's education would be affected in each of these placements. They need to know what aspects of placement are essential to their child to receive a free and appropriate education. It is only when the general concepts of continuum are related to the strengths and needs of their child do they have the knowledge to be full participants.

References

Brantlinger, E. A. (1987). Making decisions about special placement: Do low-income parents have the information they need. *Journal of Learning Disabilities, 20* (2), 84–101.

Corn, A. L., Hatlen, P., Huebner, K. M., Ryan, F., & Siller, M. A. (1995). *The national agenda for the education of children and youths with visual impairments, including those with multiple disabilities.* New York: AFB Press.

Heuman, J. (1996) Policy guidance on educating blind and visually impaired students. *RE:view, 28*(2), 71–79.

Individuals with Disabilities Education Act. (1997). 20 U. S. Congress. Chapter 33 Pub. L. 105–17. June 4, 1997.

U.S. Department of Education (1997). Nineteenth Annual Report to Congress on the Implementation of the Individuals with Disabilities Act.

Westat. (1997). OSEP IDEA, Part B data collection history. Rockville, MD: Westat.

Goal 6

Assessment of students will be conducted, in collaboration with parents, by personnel having expertise in the education of students with visual impairments.

Submitted by Lighthouse National Center for Vision and Child Development
The Lighthouse Inc., New York, NY
Prepared by Mary Ann Lang, Ph.D.
Keith Benoff, MA
Michelle Viisola, MA
Tana D'Allura, Ph.D.
Robin Leonard, MA
E. Eugenie Hartmann, Ph.D.

Background

To meet the individual needs of students, defined here as infants, toddlers, children, and adolescents with visual impairments, including those with multiple disabilities, careful and comprehensive assessment is essential. The purpose of this study was to describe what presently constitutes a comprehensive assessment for this group of students.

Assessment of students with visual impairments has been a part of the American education system for decades. Of particular importance is that these assessments be comprehensive. Academic assessment, the hallmark of educational assessment, may not be sufficient for this group of students because it does not account for their learning adaptive skills to compensate for impaired vision. Standard academic assessments may also fail to consider emotional readiness, independence skills, and communication modes. Three research questions were identified to guide this study:

1. What instruments are being used for the assessment of students with impaired vision?
2. Are assessments being conducted by personnel with expertise in the education of students with impaired vision?
3. Are parents involved in the assessment process, and if so, how?

Method

Materials

Two surveys were developed, one for professionals and one for parents. Questions for both surveys were written in 1995 by the authors in consultation with members of the Advisory Board of the Lighthouse National Center for Vision and Child Development, along with participants at the National

Agenda Advisory Board Meeting at the American Printing House for the Blind. The survey instrument for professionals included forty-five questions and was divided into several major segments. These included: comprehensive assessment, personnel, procedures for assessment, interpretation of results, and resource materials.

Questions were in various formats. Most questions initially requested a "yes" or "no" response. Some requested selection of responses from a list, with an option to check "other" and describe what "other" meant. When relevant, provision was made for single word answers to indicate how often or by whom assessments were provided. Respondents were encouraged to supply narrative responses and attach illustrations and other relevant documentation. Background information about the respondent was also requested. Surveys were provided in braille or audiotape on request. Responses were also accepted in those formats.

A second survey was prepared for parents of students with visual impairments. Questions were asked about preparation for the assessment, their role during the assessment, and feedback after the assessment. The survey instrument for parents included six questions. Two questions asked for a "yes" or "no" response. Three questions provided options to check that included "other." Two questions were open ended. In addition, respondents were encouraged to attach materials related to their responses.

Procedure

The first survey was sent to 903 professionals involved with the education of students with visual impairment. The parent survey was distributed in the Winter 1996 issue of *Awareness,* the newsletter of the National Association for Parents of the Visually Impaired (NAPVI). Surveys were returned via mail to the authors at The Lighthouse, Inc. Information was coded and analyzed using SPSS.

Results

Respondents

One hundred and thirty (14 percent) of the surveys distributed to professionals were completed and returned. Responses from those working in Head Start programs were not included because they use a different set of tests from those available to other professionals. These respondents did not constitute a significant portion of the sample and, as such, data from 118 respondents (12 percent) were used. Respondents from forty-five states representing both urban and rural communities were included.

Fifty percent of the respondents identified themselves as teachers of students with visual impairments (TVIs). Another 20 percent were administrators, half of whom reported they received training to assess students with impaired vision. Forty-seven parents responded to the study.

Comprehensive Assessment

The information contained in this section pertains only to responses provided by the respondents who were professionals.

Instruments Used for Assessments: One hundred thirty-nine assessment instruments were cited (see Tables 1 and 2). Locally developed assessment instruments were not included in Tables 1 and 2 because none were used by a significant portion of the sample. Instruments were included in Tables 1 and 2 if used by at least 5 percent of all respondents assessing at least one area. There was little consensus regarding which standardized instruments are best suited to the assessment of any area. For each area, including social development, orientation and mobility, activities of daily living, vocation, technology skills, leisure interests, learning style, environment, student and family goals, student interest, and self-concept/esteem, at least two-thirds of the time, assessments were informally performed by at least 20 percent of respondents.

Frequency of Assessments: As indicated in Table 3, fifteen of seventeen education areas were assessed at least once yearly by 40 percent or more of the respondents. Most others reported assessing the areas at least once every three years. Therefore, 80 percent of the respondents stipulated that areas were assessed at least once every three years.

Vision: The question about assessing vision asked if vision was assessed, how often, by whom, and where. A list of the tests for the assessment

Table 1 Instruments Used to Assess Psychological Areas by Percent

Instruments	Psychological	Social	Cognitive
Wechsler Tests	41	<5	23
Binet Tests	19	<5	<5
Bayley Scales	11	<5	<5
Oregon Project	6	17	32
Reynell-Zinkin	5	5	10
Woodcock-Johnson	6	<5	15
Blind Learning Aptitude Test	5	<5	5
Vineland Adaptive Behavior Scale	<5	30	<5
Denver Developmental Screening Test	6	5	<5
Social Maturity Scale	<5	8	<5
Callier-Azusa Scale	<5	8	13
Independent Living Checklists	<5	7	<5
Hawaii Early Learning Profile	<5	6	10
Battelle Development Inventory	<5	8	13
Brigance Diagnostic Inventory	<5	<5	12
Wide Range Achievement Test	<5	<5	6
Peabody Individual Achievement Test	<5	<5	6

of vision was requested. Respondents were also asked whether a diagnosis or prognosis was required prior to provision of educational services. Vision was assessed by 83 percent of all respondents. Forty-five percent assessed acuity and another 45 percent assessed functional vision; only 11 percent assessed both. Ocular diagnosis was required by 77 percent, while prognosis was required by 50 percent prior to provision of educational services.

Psychological Status: The psychological assessment addressed psychological, social, and cognitive development. A list of instruments can be found in Table 1. General psychological assessments were provided by only 54 percent of all re-

spondents, significantly less than social and cognitive development (72 percent and 70 percent) assessments. Two-thirds reported using intelligence tests to assess these areas, while only two out of ten were designed for youngsters with visual impairment. Generally, a concept development (cognitive abilities) test was used as well. The Wechsler scales were overwhelmingly the most utilized standardized tests for assessing psychological state (41 percent). The Vineland Adaptive Behavior Scale was most often chosen for assessing social development (30 percent), with the Oregon Project checklist (17 percent) next. For assessing cognitive development, the Oregon Project was cited most often (32 percent), followed by the Wechsler tests (23 percent). Because the Oregon Project is designed only for preschool age students, fewer than one-quarter of respondents who assessed cognitive development specified a standardized test for school age students.

Language: Sixty-eight percent of the respondents included a basic language assessment, performed by a speech therapist/pathologist at least 70 percent of the time. Both reading and non-reading formats, such as the Test of Language Development (19 percent) and the Peabody Picture Vocabulary Test (8 percent), respectively, were used.

Motor Skills, Mobility, and Activities of Daily Living: Details about the assessment of motor skills, mobility, and daily living skills can be found in Table 2. Two-thirds assessed motor development and mobility; three-quarters measured daily living skills. Physical or occupational therapists assessed motor development in roughly 54 percent of those assessed, while an additional 24 percent were assessed by teachers of students with visual impairments. Almost 90 percent of those who assessed mobility were orientation and mobility specialists. Daily living skills were usually assessed by teachers of students with visual impairments (42 percent). The Oregon Project (for the preschool population) was cited most often for the assessment of motor development and daily living skills. The only motor development instrument reported for older students was the Developmental Test of Visual-Motor Integration (7 percent). Assessment instruments of mobility and daily living skills for older students were

Table 2 Instruments Used to Assess Motor, Mobility, and Daily Living Areas, by Percent

Instruments	Motor	Orientation and Mobility	Activities of Daily Living
Developmental Test of Visual Motor Integration	7	<5	<5
Peabody Developmental Motor Scales	17	9	<5
Bayley Scales	5	<5	5
Oregon Project	29	<5	18
Reynell-Zinkin	<5	<5	5
Test of Sensory Integration	5	6	<5
Carolina Developmental Profile	5	<5	<5
Vineland Adaptive Behavior Scale	<5	5	12
Denver Developmental Screening Test	7	<5	<5
Cratty & Sams Test of Body Image of Blind Children	<5	11	<5
Callier-Azusa Scale	11	<5	5
Independent Living Checklists	<5	20	15
Hawaii Early Learning Profile	9	5	6
Battelle Development Inventory	9	<5	8
Brigance Diagnostic Inventory	<5	<5	5
Hill Performance Test of Selected Positional Concepts	<5	15	<5

Table 3 Frequency of Assessment by Percent of Areas Assessed

Area Assessed	Once Yearly	Once Every Three Years	When Requested	Once	Not Specified
Vision	46	24	9	2	19
Medical	46	16	18	16	4
Psychological	11	73	13	2	1
Social development	46	42	7	0	5
Language	41	30	26	0	3
Cognitive development	44	43	11	0	2
Motor development	49	23	23	0	5
Orientation & mobility	49	28	18	1	4
Activities of daily living	57	20	17	2	4
Vocation	42	12	19	16	11
Technology skills	33	4	58	1	4
Leisure interests	40	25	24	4	7
Learning styles	40	32	23	2	3
Home environment	47	15	16	2	20
Student/family goals	83	6	2	3	6
Student's interest	67	12	12	3	6
Self-concept/esteem	43	26	31	0	0

used more frequently. The Independent Living Checklist was used to assess mobility development by 20 percent of the respondents and daily living skills by 15 percent of the respondents.

Vocational Interests: Forty-nine percent of the respondents performed vocational interests assess-ments. Considering that fewer than 25 percent work exclusively with children under seven years, almost half did not assess those students who would be old enough to be exploring vocations. Of those who assessed vocational interests, fewer than 5 percent specified any instrument.

Technology Skills: Fifty-eight percent performed technology skills assessments, mostly on request. Technology teachers performed assessments 23 percent of the time, and teachers of students with visual impairments performed assessments 53 percent of the time. Six percent assessed students' ability to use computers and various software, 5 percent assessed students' ability to use closed-circuit televisions in addition to computers. Of those who assessed technology skills, fewer than 5 percent specified any instrument.

Personnel

Personnel Responsible for Providing Assessments: Responses indicated that assessment was performed by a wide range of professionals and para-professionals, most often in school or at the student's home. As indicated in Table 4, at least 25 percent of the time, the teachers of students with visual impairments are most frequently responsible for the assessment of all areas, with four exceptions: orientation and mobility, language development, medical history, and psychological state. For these areas, a specialist (e.g., an orientation and mobility instructor) performs the assessments. It is noteworthy that for social development, a psychosocial area, the teacher of students with visual impairments was responsible more often than a psychologist; for cognitive development, the teacher of students with visual impairments assessed students with comparable frequency.

Training: Thirty-eight percent of respondents received ongoing training related to the assessment of students with visual impairment: 27 percent attended in-service training or workshops; 5 percent attended state-mandated training sessions. Fifty-three percent received training for the interpretation of results and development of educational plans; 37 percent attended in-service training or workshops, while 6 percent received instructional seminars from local schools for the blind. In the absence of formalized training, 4 percent worked with colleagues to gain experience.

Procedures for Assessment

Parental Notification and Involvement: Data related to parental notification, preparation for, and involvement in the assessment are presented in Table 5. Most notable is the difference in reported involvement between parents and professionals. Professionals responded that they notify parents of an assessment 93 percent of the time and prepared parents for the assessment 89 percent of the time. Parents, on the other hand, reported that they were notified only 73 percent of the time and prepared 60 percent of the time. Professionals indicated that they asked parents for background information for 59 percent of all assessments and provided feedback 20 percent of the time. Parents responded that they provided background information only 41 percent of the time and were given feedback following assessments 25 percent of the time. In addition, 75 percent of the professionals reported assessing parental satisfaction with the assessment, whereas parents claimed to be asked only 52 percent of the time.

Translation: When parents do not speak English, 54 percent of professionals indicated that interpreters were provided. Fourteen percent of the respondents also stated that they provide printed material in several languages for parents to take home and read. Twenty-four percent had not yet had to deal with foreign languages and did not provide information as to how they would deal with this situation.

Assessment Obstacles: Thirty-nine percent of the respondents felt that there were no major obstacles to providing a comprehensive assessment. Twelve percent specified a lack of appropriate psychological and technological assessment instruments, while 13 percent specified staffing and financial limitations. Others (6 percent) mentioned physical and mental limitations of the children. Finally, 5 percent specified difficulty reaching parents to obtain permission to assess children. Although 61 percent felt there were significant obstacles to a complete assessment, 56 percent were content with the assessments they performed. Six percent suggested that a more complete vision assessment was needed. Five percent specified a need for more comprehensive vocational interests assessment instruments. Six percent specified a need to assess daily living skills, while 4 percent felt it important to assess orientation and mobility skills. Others expressed an interest in more effectively assessing language, learning styles, speech, and self-esteem. The survey did not ask about nutrition

Table 4 Personnel Responsible for Assessment of Students with Visual Impairments, by Percent

	Teacher of the Visually Impaired	Psychologist	Classroom Teacher	O&M Teacher	SPED Teacher	Physical Therapist	Other	Physician/ Nurse
Vision	35	0	2	2	0	0	24	37
Medical	1	0	1	0	0	0	9	89
Psychological	8	79	2	0	0	0	11	0
Social development	29	19	16	1	0	0	35	0
Language	16	4	5	0	1	0	74	0
Cognitive development	34	41	7	1	7	0	10	0
Motor development	24	4	9	0	1	40	22	0
Orientation & mobility	7	0	1	88	1	2	0	1
Activities of daily living	42	9	13	4	2	3	26	1
Vocation	29	9	9	1	1	0	51	0
Technology skills	54	0	9	1	0	0	35	1
Leisure interests	49	2	29	0	4	2	14	0
Learning styles	52	17	28	0	3	0	0	0
Home environment	21	1	10	22	2	0	43	1
Student/family goals	29	4	39	0	16	0	12	0
Student's interest	26	3	29	2	16	0	23	1
Self-concept/esteem	26	28	23	0	6	0	17	0

or sexual knowledge assessments, but several respondents indicated that these areas should be assessed.

Fourteen percent expressed a need for intelligence tests designed for and standardized on students with visual impairments. Five percent also asked for visual assessment tests. Of those using standardized tests, 65 percent record standardized results, while 80 percent had no coding system for nonstandardized test results.

Interpretation of Assessment Results

In addition to providing information during the preparation stages of assessments, teachers of students with visual impairments have also observed and provided feedback for 84 percent of the assessments. Their expertise was requested 88 percent of the time to link observations to formal test data. When interpretations of test data were to be used in the development of recommendations, teachers of students with visual impairments were consulted 65 percent of the time. Following the assessments, 44 percent of the professionals re-

ported sending results to parents and meeting personally to review them, while 38 percent sent no material but met with the parents. About 4 percent sent a copy of the report in place of a personal conference, while 7 percent did not specify how they reviewed their findings with parents. Parents stated that they were given reports 21 percent of the time or met personally fifty percent of the time.

Fifty-five percent of the professionals reported that they sent material to and met in person with other professionals, while 21 percent arranged in-person conferences and 7 percent only sent materials to other professionals. Nine percent did not specify how they shared information with other professionals.

Discussion

This survey was designed to describe the current state of assessment of students with visual impairment, including those with multiple disabilities. Three major themes requiring attention seem to emerge.

Table 5 Parental Notification, Preparation for, and Involvement in Assessment, by Percent

	Parent Report	Professional Report
Parental Notification		
Overall notification	73	93
Telephone call only	23	Not specified
Mail only	27	Not specified
In-person meeting only	8	14
Mail and telephone call	Not specified	52
Parental Preparation		
Overall preparation	60	89
Sending material and meeting personally	15	18
Meeting personally only	50	24
Personal and telephone conferences	Not specified	14
Sending material, calling and meeting personally	Not specified	33
Calling only	8	Not specified
Sending material only	6	Not specified
Parental Role During Assessment		
Background information	41	59
Provide feedback during assessment	25	20
Participate in program design	Not specified	14
Parental Satisfaction Review		
Overall satisfaction review	52	75
Meeting personally	15	12
Surveys	Not specified	14
Ask at IEP conference	Not specified	17
Means of review not specified	10	36

1. What is assessed.
2. What assessment instruments are used.
3. What type of assessment training is needed.

These themes are related to the three primary research questions.

Areas Assessed

There is considerable variability in what was assessed. For example, over 70 percent of respondents assessed vision, social abilities, motor skills, orientation and mobility, activities of daily living, cognition, leisure skills, and family goals. On the other hand, less than half assessed color vision, visual perception, medical status, learning style, or vocational skills. And, finally, only half provided psychological, language, visual acuity, functional vision, technology, environmental, student interest, or self-concept/esteem assessment. Because there are no standards which indicate which areas must be assessed for children with visual impairments, one can only comment at this time regarding the extent to which assessments are provided in different areas.

Assessment Instruments

One hundred thirty-nine standardized tests as well as locally developed tests and checklists were used. Although a systematic analysis of the instruments is not yet complete, it is clear that several standardized tests were used for purposes other than those for which they were developed and with populations for which they were not intended. For example, the Wechsler tests were employed by 41 percent of respondents to assess general psychological state. These tests were often adapted by eliminating all performance subtests. Even after this adjustment, several of the remaining questions are visually oriented. In addition, aspects of intellectual development may be overlooked. Goldman (1970) posits that the exclusive use of verbal sections fails to tap the abilities most important to individuals with visual impairments. As such, a scarcity of appropriate assessment material was reported by 12 percent of respondents as a major obstacle to a complete assessment. For all areas assessed, at least 30 percent of the respondents either did not specify an instrument or specified informal observations as a means of assessment. Additionally, with the exception of a few instruments, such as the Wechsler tests for cognition and the Independent Living Checklist for orientation and mobility, fewer than 20 percent of respondents specified any one instrument for a particular area. The frequency of observational assessment, locally developed but not validated instruments, and the lack of consensus regarding standardized tests point to the need for a standard protocol for areas to be assessed and instruments used. This protocol must also be subject to modification according to the individual needs and degree of impairment of each student.

Assessment Training

Those charged with assessing students with visual impairments and multiple disabilities require specialized training in determining what areas should be assessed and how the assessments should be performed. Almost 50 percent of the professionals who indicated they were responsible for most areas of assessment are teachers of students with visual impairments. When assessing students with visual disabilities, psychologists, social workers, and regular education teachers independently adapted materials designed to evaluate sighted students. They created modifications often without the benefit of any additional training in the assessment of students with visual impairments. Only 37 percent of the professionals who responded to the survey reported attending in-service training or workshops designed to advise professionals of new developments and materials.

Limitations of the Study

Ideally, the professional to whom the survey was addressed filled out all questions after consulting with others responsible for assessment in areas beyond his or her domain. However, in some cases, the respondent completed the survey, leaving out information in areas for which the respondent was not responsible. In most cases where the respondent answered questions about areas outside his or her domain, all requested data was provided except the nature or title of the assessment instruments used.

A compendium of assessment instruments used by the respondents for the areas assessed is incomplete at this time. Therefore, evaluative statements regarding the use of assessment instruments should be considered with caution. Statements were made based on impressions of background material.

Inconsistencies between parent and clinician reports regarding notification and review of assessments may result from differences in perceptions. Both parents and professionals specified meetings or telephone consultation with professionals to discuss the assessment. By the assessors' admission, consultation was brief due to limited time availability. Parents may have felt that they were not afforded appropriate time to have their questions and concerns addressed, leading them to believe they were not prepared for an assessment, nor was their satisfaction with the assessment solicited.

Implications

The following suggestions seem warranted from the information derived from this survey. There is a need to:

1. Prepare and disseminate guidelines concerning areas to be assessed and appropriate instruments for assessing each area.
2. Evaluate instruments currently used, outlining positive and negative attributes.
3. Prepare and disseminate guidelines for adapting assessment instruments and interpreting results when adaptations are made.
4. Develop and publicize existing training programs for professionals who conduct and interpret assessments.

References

Goldman, H. (1970). Psychological testing of blind children. *American Foundation for the Blind Research Bulletin, 21*, 77–90.

Addendum
Instruments Most Frequently Used for Assessment of Students with Visual Impairments

Battelle Development Inventory
Bayley Scales of Infant Development, Second Edition
Blind Learning Aptitude Test
Brigance Diagnostic Inventory of Early Development
Callier-Azusa Scale: G Edition

Carolina Curriculum for Handicapped Infants and Infants at Risk

Denver Developmental Screening Test

Developmental Test of Visual Motor Integration, Third Edition

Hawaii Early Learning Profile

Hill Performance Test of Selected Positional Concepts

Independent Living: A Curriculum with Adaptations for Students with Visual Impairments. Volume 1: Social Competence, Second Edition

Independent Living: A Curriculum with Adaptations for Students with Visual Impairments. Volume 2: Self-Care and Maintenance of Personal Environment, Second Edition

Oregon Project for Visually Impaired and Blind Preschool Children

Peabody Developmental Motor Scales and Activity Cards

Peabody Individual Achievement Test

Perkins-Binet Test of Intelligence for the Blind

Reynell-Zinkin Scales: Developmental Scale for Young Visually Handicapped Children

Social Maturity Scale for Blind Preschool Children

Test of Sensory Integration

The Body Image of Blind Children

Vineland Adaptive Behavior Scale

Wechsler Adult Intelligence Scale-R

Wechsler Intelligence Scale for Children-III

Wide Range Achievement Test

Woodcock-Johnson Psycho-Educational Battery—Revised

Related Reading

Ammerman, R. T., Van Hasselt, V. B., & Hersen, M. (1986). Psychological adjustment of visually handicapped children and youth. *Clinical Psychology Review, 6*, 67–85.

Brigance, A. H. (1991). *Brigance Diagnostic Inventory of Early Development*. North Billerica, MA: Curriculum Associates, Inc.

Burlingham, D. (1965). Some problems of ego development in blind children. *Psychological Study of the Child, 19*, 95–112.

Corn, A. L., Hatlen, P., Huebner, K. M., Ryan, F., & Siller, M. A. (1995). *The national agenda for the education of children and youths with visual impairments, including those with multiple disabilities.* New York: AFB Press.

Cratty, B. J., & Sams, T. A. (1968). *The body image of blind children.* New York: American Foundation for the Blind.

Davis, C. J. (1980). *Perkins-Binet test of intelligence for the blind.* Watertown, MA: Perkins School for the Blind.

Dunn, L. M., Robertson, G. J., & Eisenberg, J. L. (1981). *The Peabody picture vocabulary test.* Circle Pines, MN: American Guidance Service.

Furuno, S., O'Reilly, K. A., Hosaka, C. M., Inatsuka, T. T., Zeisloft-Falbey, B., & Allman, T. (1988). *Hawaii early learning profile.* Palo Alto, CA: VORT Corporation.

Hammill, D. D., & Newcomer, P. L. (1988). *Test of language development.* Austin, TX: PRO-Ed.

Hill, E. W. (1981). *Hill performance test of selected positional concepts.* Wood Dale, IL: Stoelting Company.

Landau, B. (1983). Blind children's language is not "meaningless." In A. E. Mills (Ed.), *Language acquisition in the blind child: Normal and deficient* (pp. 62–76). London: Croom Helm.

Loumiet, R., & Levack, N. (1991). *Independent living: A curriculum with adaptations for students with visual impairments.* Austin: Texas School for the Blind and Visually Impaired.

Maxfield, K. E., & Buchholz, S. (1958). *Social maturity scale for blind preschool children.* New York: American Foundation for the Blind.

Newland, T. E. (1964). Prediction and evaluation of academic learning by blind children. *International Journal for the Education of the Blind, 14*, 1–7.

Newland, T. E. (1971). *Blind learning aptitude test.* Champaign: University of Illinois Press.

Reynell, J., & Zinkin, P. (1979). *Reynell-Zinkin scales: Developmental scale for young visually handicapped children.* London: NFER-Nelson Publishing.

Sparrow, S. S., Balia, D. A. & Cicchetti, D. V. (1984). *Vineland adaptive behavior scale.* Circle Pines, MN: American Guidance Services.

Van Hasselt, V. B. (1983). Social adaptation in the blind. *Clinical Psychology Review, 3*, 87–107.

Van Hasselt, V. B., Kazdin, A. E., Hersen, H., Simon, J., & Mastantuones, A. K. (1985). A behavioral-analytic model for assessing social skills in blind adolescents. *Behavior Research and Therapy, 23*, 395–405.

Warren, D. H. (1994). *Blindness and children: An individual differences approach.* Cambridge: Cambridge University Press.

Wechsler, D. (1991). *Wechsler intelligence scale for children* (3rd ed.). San Antonio, TX: The Psychological Corporation.

Williams, C. E. (1978). Strategies of intervention with the profoundly retarded visually-handicapped child: A brief report of a study of stereotypy. *Occasional Papers of the British Psychological Society, 2*, 68–72.

Woodcock, R. W., Johnson, B. M., Mather, N., McGrew, K. S., & Werder, J. K. (1991). *Woodcock-Johnson psycho-educational battery—Revised.* Chicago: Riverside Publishing Company.

Goal 7

Access to developmental and educational services will include an assurance that instructional materials are available to students in the appropriate media and at the same time as their sighted peers.

Submitted by the Association of Instructional Resource Centers for the Visually Handicapped (AIRCVH)
Prepared by Suzanne A. Dalton

Background and Related Information

At its annual meeting in October 1995, the Association of Instructional Resource Centers for the Visually Handicapped (AIRCVH) agreed to assume responsibility for the implementation of Goal 7. AIRCVH members divided into small groups to develop specific questions that would be included on a national survey to determine the current status of production and acquisition of specialized materials. Members of the National Agenda Advisory Board offered additional suggestions about the survey instruments at the National Agenda meeting on June 10, 1996.

Procedure

With the suggested items incorporated, the Goal 7 Survey was distributed to each state on July 22, 1996, with a return deadline of September 15, 1996. The cover memorandum requested that each state submit only *one* completed survey form

to eliminate duplication of information. To assist with that request, each cover memorandum listed the names of the other individuals in their state who had received the survey. Most states complied with the request to submit one completed survey.

Instruments and Respondents

The survey instrument consisted of thirty-two questions separated into two sections addressing: (1) the provision of materials and (2) the quality of materials. The instrument and specific results are provided in Appendix B.

Sample or Subjects

The survey was distributed to AIRCVH members, "friends" of AIRCVH (included in the AIRCVH mailing list), superintendents of residential schools, and the National Agenda State Coordinators. Of the 150 surveys distributed, thirty survey responses were received. Responses represented information from the following twenty-seven states: Alaska, Arizona, Arkansas, California (partial), Colorado (partial), Florida, Georgia, Idaho, Indiana, Iowa, Kansas, Maryland, Massachusetts, Minnesota, Missouri, New Mexico, North Carolina, Ohio, Oregon, Pennsylvania (partial), South Carolina, South Dakota, Vermont, Virginia, Washington, Wyoming, and West Virginia. The analysis of the data was conducted on information received from 54 percent of the states.

Analysis of Data

Section I: Provision of Materials

Analysis of the data from the 27 states revealed that 25,000 students with visual impairments were receiving specialized services. The majority of the responding states served students enrolled in public, residential, private, and adult education programs. Eleven of the states have an official state policy granting copyright permission for transcription of specialized materials.

The $3.5 million expended annually from the represented states for producing specialized materials were generated from the following three sources: Federal quota funds (42 percent); Individuals with Disabilities Education Act (IDEA) Part B funds (16 percent); and individual state funds (42 percent). Five states received funds from foundations; four states sold specialized materials to other states; and one state received money from a volunteer group. Fourteen states utilize trained volunteers to produce an estimated twelve million dollars' worth of materials. Seven states utilize programs at state or federal prisons to prepare materials in accessible format.

The average time span between the initial materials order and completed materials delivery varied according to the time of year. In May, the average time span is four and one-half to five weeks; in July it is six and one-half to seven weeks; and in September it is five and one-half to six weeks. The states track this information by using computers with commercial or customized software. About half of the represented states loan materials to other states with an average of three to five titles per year.

On September 15 of any given school year, fourteen states indicated that 81 to 100 percent of their students needed specialized materials. Factors that influence delivery timelines include late orders, lack of sources, lack of money, late text adoption timelines by local education agencies (LEAs), subject matter ordered, copyright permission problems, student scheduling, new students, and length of braille production process. To avoid delayed materials delivery, states encourage early ordering, send reminder correspondence, and reiterate standards such as those in free appropriate public education (FAPE) regulations, Individual Education Programs, and braille legislation statutes.

In the provision of *braille materials,* the majority of the represented states fill orders in the following percentage categories: 0 to 20 percent via quota funds; 21 to 40 percent via outside vendors; 21 to 40 percent via in-stock items; 0 to 20 percent via internal production; 0 to 20 percent via borrowed items; and 0 to 20 percent represent canceled orders.

For *large-print materials,* the majority of the represented states fill orders in the following percentage categories: 0 to 20 percent via quota funds; 0 to 20 percent via outside vendors; 21 to 40 percent via in-stock items; 21 to 40 percent via internal production; 0 to 20 percent via borrowed items; and 0 to 20 percent represent canceled orders.

In providing *recorded materials,* the majority of the represented states fill orders in the following percentage categories: 0 to 20 percent via quota funds; 0 to 20 percent via outside vendors; 0 to 20 percent via in-stock items; 0 to 20 percent via internal pro-

duction; 81 to 100 percent via borrowed items; and 0 to 20 percent represent canceled orders.

For *electronic format,* the majority of represented states did not provide these materials to students.

In the provision of *educational aids including materials for those with multiple disabilities,* the majority of the represented states fill orders in the following percentage categories: 21 to 80 percent via quota funds; 0 to 20 percent via outside vendors; 21 to 40 percent via in-stock items; negligible via internal production; 0 to 20 percent via borrowed items; and 0 to 20 percent represent canceled orders.

Twelve states offer access to low vision evaluations and to optical devices, with five states providing the same services to students with multiple disabilities. Three states require learning media assessments that can lead to a low vision referral. The LEA, parents, or the state rehabilitation agency pay for the majority of low vision services and devices. Two states have organized regularly scheduled low vision clinics and five provide statewide low vision services to the school-age population through clinics housed at the residential school.

The following states submitted copies of state laws and/or education policies relating to the provision of specialized materials for students with visual impairments: Arizona, Arkansas, California, Florida, Georgia, Indiana, Kansas, New Mexico, Ohio, Oregon, and Virginia.

Section II: Quality of Materials

Of the eighteen states that use volunteers to produce specialized materials, the majority require Library of Congress certification and utilize the following standards/guidelines: Literary Code, Textbook Code, Nemeth Code, Music Code, Computer Code, National Braille Association (NBA), and Braille Authority of North America (BANA). A few states use standards established by the California Transcribers and Educators of the Visually Handicapped (CTEVH) or by individual volunteer groups.

Even though eleven states utilize "quick and dirty" braille, these states indicate that the "quick and dirty" braille represents only 0 to 10 percent of their braille production. Usually these materials are produced at the request of a certified teacher of students with visual impairments. Seventeen of twenty states indicated that tactile graphics were routinely included in texts. The majority of states utilize Library of Congress, NBA, or BANA guidelines in the production of tactile graphics.

In the production of braille, accuracy is assured via the use of proofreaders in fifteen states. Seven states employ software to proofread materials. Generally, the state education agency (SEA) or the instructional resource center (IRC) will pay for the proofreading. Ten states also conduct an annual formal/informal survey of teachers, administrators, and users to collect additional data concerning the quality of materials. Large-print and recorded texts are generally spot-checked by states rather than proofread.

For purchasing specialized materials, the following criteria are used in the selection of a supplier: price of materials, appropriate format, speed of delivery/turnaround time, overall quality of braille output, availability, reputation of vendor, and whether or not the item is available on quota. In the majority of states, the quality of materials is reviewed annually via a formal/informal survey of teachers, administrators, and users.

Implications and Discussion

The Goal 7 survey revealed very few surprises to individuals currently providing specialized materials to students with visual impairments. It is apparent that instructional materials can and are offered to our students in specialized formats, but these instructional materials certainly are *not* provided *at the same time* as those for their sighted peers. Timely materials delivery can be adversely affected by unpredictable occurrences—such as family, mobility, or weather disasters. It can also be affected by factors that can somewhat be controlled—such as late textbook adoption timelines by LEAs, lack of sources for Nemeth materials, lack of money, site-based decision making at individual school level, and copyright permission problems. These latter factors should serve as the focus of future efforts for achieving Goal 7.

It is apparent that the majority of individuals and organizations producing specialized materials utilize the Library of Congress, the National Braille Association (NBA), and the Braille Authority of North America (BANA) standards. In the production of tactile graphics, the use of standardized guidelines is less clear. Another challenge facing our field is the need to standardize the generation of tactile graphics.

Access to low vision evaluations for students with visual impairments is another area of concern. Only twelve of twenty-seven states provided systematic access to low vision evaluations. Of greater concern is that only five of twenty-seven states offered systematic access to low vision evaluations to students with multiple disabilities. The five states that provided statewide low vision services to the school-age population did so through clinics housed at the residential school. It is suggested that other states consider implementing the residential school model of providing statewide low vision evaluations to the school-age population including those students with multiple disabilities.

Recommendations for Further Research

At the 1997 Josephine L. Taylor Leadership Institute, twenty-one participants in the Education Work Group reviewed Goal 7's survey results and drafted *Report to the Nation*. Consumers, educators, parents, students, and instructional resource center staff participated in these discussions. The Work Group offered the following recommendations:

1. Establish guidelines for staffing statewide and/or regional centers that produce specialized materials.
2. Ensure access to all instructional materials by creating uniform access standards for texts in braille, large-print, recorded, electronic, descriptive video, and on-line formats.
3. Offer needed accommodation that ensures access to assistive technology in the classroom for all students with visual impairments.
4. Establish guidelines that will promote standardization in the production of tactile graphics.
5. Encourage vendors to continue ongoing research and development related to full-page tactile displays.
6. Continue to communicate with textbook publishers promoting their provision of texts in accessible media.

These six recommendations were presented to the AIRCVH membership during their 1997 Annual Meeting.

Goal 8

Educational and developmental goals, including instruction, will reflect the assessed needs of each student in all areas of academic and disability-specific core curricula.

Submitted by the Texas School for the Blind and Visually Impaired
Prepared by Phil Hatlen, Ed.D.

Background

Educators of blind and visually impaired students have known for some time that children have instructional needs that extend beyond the academic curriculum. These include concepts, tasks, and behaviors learned largely through incidental visual observation. The first of these officially recognized by the profession was orientation and mobility. Other areas, such as independent living skills, career education, and low vision utilization, are also identified as unique learning needs. These were often added to the learning needs of students and taught as time allowed. Seldom did skills in independent living receive the same priority as learning to read. Some professionals question the existing system, which requires academics but relegates these other skills and knowledge areas to a category of "related" or "elective." Goal 8 seeks to remove the myth of this double standard by identifying and delivering a core curriculum that is specifically tailored to the

educational needs of students who are visually impaired.

Procedure

The participants of the 1995 Josephine L. Taylor Leadership Institute developed strategies to achieve the goals of the National Agenda. The recommended national strategies have guided the work on this goal for the last two years. One recommendation was to clearly define, develop, and disseminate the disability-specific core curriculum areas for students with visual impairments, including those with multiple disabilities.

In response, the first draft of "The Core Curriculum for Blind and Visually Impaired Students, Including Those with Additional Disabilities" was developed. It was disseminated widely, first to the National Agenda Goal Leaders, Advisory Board, and State Coordinators. Revisions and additions were made and by the fall of 1995, the final form of the document was completed. Educators now had, in writing, a clear and comprehensive statement identifying the fundamental educational needs of students with visual impairments. Dissemination began with the publication of an article in the Spring 1996 issue of *RE:view*. At the same time, the core curriculum document was part of a packet of National Agenda information disseminated through State Coordinators. A total of 2,000 packets was distributed nationwide.

Another recommendation was to create annotated bibliographies, related to the core curriculum, available either in hard copy or through electronic means to professionals and parents. A first draft of an annotated bibliography has been completed. It provides information and sources for both assessment and instruction in all core curriculum areas specific to students with visual impairments and is available from the Texas School for the Blind and Visually Impaired.

Another recommendation was to work to obtain formal adoption of the disability-specific core curriculum by national organizations of professionals and others. At its biennial convention in the summer of 1996, the Association for Education and Rehabilitation of the Blind and Visually Impaired (AER) passed a resolution endorsing the core curriculum. Presentations on the core curriculum have been and continue to be made throughout the country. More formal endorsements will be sought. It was expected that the dissemination of the National Agenda packets to State Coordinators, which included the core curriculum, would result in state and regional endorsements, but there is no evidence that this has happened.

Survey Conducted

The National Goal Leader (NGL) for Goal 8 was unable to launch a comprehensive, national study of the current level of instruction in the core curriculum. A small survey was made of teachers asking them to respond to questions about acceptance and implementation of the core curriculum. Along with the questionnaire, teachers were provided with a copy of the paper on the core curriculum. State Coordinators for the National Agenda in ten selected states were asked to distribute a questionnaire to ten teachers in their respective states. The questionnaires were mailed back to the NGL.

It was assumed that teachers had accepted the necessity of implementing the core curriculum for all students with visual impairments. Therefore, the questionnaire consisted of only three items:

1. Are you able to assess and instruct, as appropriate, in all areas of this core curriculum for your students? Please consider all students on your caseload, including those with additional disabilities.
2. If not, what are the barriers you face in addressing all areas of this curriculum in the IEPs for your students? Are any particular curricular topics more difficult to include in your instructional day?
3. What are your suggestions on how to overcome those barriers?

The return from a potential sample of 100 was twenty-five. Although a sample of this size representing the entire country is not acceptable, the data received is believed to provide information that would be constant, regardless of sample size. In response to item 1, nine teachers answered "yes" and sixteen "no." When asked about barriers to providing the core curriculum, the following responses occurred more than four times:

a. Caseload too large
b. Must first meet academic needs
c. Inadequate assessment materials
d. No recognition of need from administration
e. Students do not have enough time

Suggestions for overcoming these barriers included:

a. Summer programs
b. Schools for the blind
c. Extended year/extended day
d. In-service for administrators and teachers in denial
e. More placement options

Implications and Discussion

This survey uncovered no real surprises. In fact, barriers and potential solutions are what one might expect as responses to the questions. The results add additional evidence that what professionals and parents have experienced for many years is, in fact, probably true. Many children are not receiving the core curriculum because teachers are carrying caseloads that are too large and do not give the teacher ample time to do much more than be an academic tutor. It has been a common story told by teachers that they are expected to keep children on target with their classmates in academic subjects, and only if there is additional time is the expanded core curriculum to be considered. Most urgent, perhaps, is the teacher's inability to address the core curriculum because administrators do not recognize its importance. A strategy of the National Agenda for implementation must be the in-servicing of administrators and policy makers.

For ways in which these barriers might be overcome, it is obvious that creative and imaginative planning must take place so that we do not end up with programs that keep children in school for ten to twelve hours per day. New approaches must be found to provide instruction, and new designs for service delivery must be developed. The goal is to provide instruction in all core curriculum areas. We will need to expand our thinking, leave old models behind, and look for innovative and individualized ways to better serve children. Only then will we attain Goal 8.

The Future

1. Completion and dissemination of annotated bibliographies on all areas of the core curriculum.

2. Adoption of the core curriculum by state departments of education and other general educators in key positions.

3. Work with personnel preparation programs to assure that future teachers are being prepared to teach all areas of the core curriculum.

4. Collaborate with future endeavors that assess the implementation of the core curriculum with students. A proposal currently under review calls for:

. . . a three-phase project to investigate the degree to which the Expanded Core Curriculum is being taught by teachers of students with visual impairment.

STATE REPORTS

For each state, one or more individuals volunteered to serve as State Coordinator. Several states have followed the national model of having co-chairs consisting of a parent and a professional. In preparation for this *Report to the Nation,* all state coordinators were invited to submit summary reports of National Agenda activities within their state. The following information was reported by National Agenda State Coordinators for twenty-eight states and reflects some activities that have occurred in these states up to the spring of 1997.

Arkansas—Reported by Bob Brasher and Cay Holbrook. The Arkansas team developed the "Arkansas Agenda." Using the National Agenda, the team assessed the state's current status, strengths, and weaknesses. They developed steps to achieve the eight goals and distributed this information along with the National Agenda public information packets. These packets were distributed throughout the state for the purpose of obtaining state organizations' endorsements. The team secured additional endorsements from state institutions such as the University of Arkansas, Little Rock, and Services for the Blind, as well as parent and community service organizations. The Arkansas Agenda includes state-specific goals and the steps needed to achieve them. Each goal has an identified goal leader and organizational partners working together toward the goal. Because the plan is extensive, just a few of the state goals and the steps to achieve them are listed here.

Arkansas Goal 1: Timely referral—Students and their families will be referred to appropriate services at the Arkansas School for the Blind (ASB)/Educational Services for Visually Impaired (ESVI) within thirty days of identification of a sus-

pected visual impairment. Steps to achieve this goal include: (1) develop procedures for tracking referrals; (2) disseminate information about visual impairments to local hospitals, ophthalmologists, clinics, etc.; (3) establish cooperative efforts with early childhood coordinators; (4) increase regional parent contacts; (5) speak to early childhood/special education classes at all state universities; (6) publish the ASB phone number in all local Arkansas phone directories.

Arkansas Goal 2: Parent involvement—Policies and procedures will be implemented to ensure the rights of all parents to full participation and equal partnership in the education process. Steps to achieve this goal include the provision of: braille classes for parents, orientation for parents about all services available, increased parent information (in alternative formats for those who do not read print), regional ASB meetings, and parent representatives at ASB staff and teacher meetings.

Arkansas Goal 8: Core curriculum—Educational and developmental goals, including instruction, will reflect the assessed needs of each student in all areas of academic and disability-specific core curriculum. Steps to achieve this goal include: (1) disseminate information about the core curriculum to appropriate professionals; (2) develop procedures for determining the need for specialized instruction for students with visual impairments; (3) develop guidelines and justifications for service to students with low vision; and (4) determine the availability of specialized instruction in all service delivery systems.

California—Reported by Stephen A. Goodman. California has established "Californians Working to Achieve the National Agenda." The group's first objective was to focus attention on the National Agenda within existing statewide organizations and agencies. In addition, an effort was made to secure maximum involvement of educators, parents, and consumers at both individual and organizational levels. Additional endorsements have been obtained and a "California Summit on Blindness and Visual Impairment: Putting It All Together" was organized by California's Joint Action Committee of Organizations Serving the Visually Impaired (JAC) and the Low Incidence Disability Advisory Committee (LIDAC). This summit was held in conjunction with the thirty-eighth Annual Conference of the California Transcribers and Educators of the Visually Handicapped. The focus of the summit included the establishment of goals, data collection, and development of position papers relative to the most critical issues affecting visually impaired Californians of all ages. The issues identified were personnel preparation and caseload sizes.

Florida—Reported by Carol Allman. Florida has developed a state strategic plan addressing actions currently in place to accomplish the National Agenda goals. The Department of Education is dedicating one of its set-aside "Weekend with the Experts" sessions to develop teacher/parent workgroups that will advocate for and promote achievement of the goals. Florida's state plan addresses each of the eight goals with contact information for the organizations assuming primary responsibility for implementing activities specific to each goal. Some examples follow.

Goal 3: Personnel Preparation—Universities, with a minimum of one full-time faculty member in the area of visual impairment, will prepare a sufficient number of educators of students with visual impairments to meet personnel needs throughout the country. Steps to achieve this goal include: (1) Florida State University (FSU), Department of Special Education, will continue to provide undergraduate and graduate programs in the areas of orientation and mobility, teacher preparation, visually impaired/multiple handicaps and rehabilitation teaching; (2) staff at the FSU Vision program will be increased by one faculty member in 1997. Currently three staff and two adjunct faculty provide the visual disabilities program.

Goal 4: Service providers will determine caseloads based on the needs of students and will require ongoing professional development for all teachers and orientation and mobility instructors. Steps to achieve this goal include: (1) teachers and orientation mobility instructors are encouraged to monitor their caseloads to assure that appropriate services are given to all students, and issues on caseloads are brought to the attention of the program specialist of children with visual impairments; (2) proposed funding models are reviewed and field testing is monitored at the state level to assure appropriate service delivery, funding levels, and caseloads for students in programs for students with visual impairments.

Georgia—Reported by Faye Mullis Taylor and Richard E. Hyer, Jr. During the annual workshop for teachers of students with visual impairments, held at the Georgia Academy for the Blind, a proclamation of support for the National Agenda was signed by the teacher/consultant of the Local Education Agenda Resource Center (LEARC). A pledge was made to develop a state plan, along with a commitment that the Academy would also create a plan specific to the school. In addition, the parents of students at the Academy were oriented to the National Agenda through distribution of the National Agenda booklet at the time of school registration and through other faculty efforts.

Iowa—Reported by Dotta Hassman. Iowa has been active in its work on the National Agenda goals by addressing several goals through specific activities. Goal 4, which involves caseload sizes and ongoing professional development, was the basis for an Itinerant Teachers' Workshop resulting in the creation of a core committee to write new state guidelines. The committee includes parents, administrators, and other professionals. The Association of Service Providers for the Visually Impaired is meeting regularly to assess education programming for Iowa students as addressed in Goals 5 and 6. A survey of students was conducted in three area education agencies concerning achievement rates of IEP goals and will contribute to the assessment component of the state guidelines. Goal 8, core curriculum, is being used to support programming recommendations and Goal 3 is being addressed through a grant application with the University of Alabama for bringing a teacher training program to Iowa. State Vision Screening Guidelines were completed and disseminated to improve referral as addressed in Goal 1. Goal 7, appropriate media, was addressed through the implementation of a statewide grant for technology for students who use braille as a learning medium. The technology includes speech, braille, and print access at forty-two Iowa locations.

Kansas—Reported by William Daugherty. The chair of the state's effort reports that the first year was devoted to dissemination of information about the National Agenda to education administrators and policy makers throughout the state. This information was also shared with parent groups and other professionals. At the 1997 AER Kansas Conference, work groups addressed the most pressing needs and determined strategies for achieving the respective goals.

Kentucky—Reported by Linda Smith. Kentuckians have taken many opportunities during state conferences, workshops, and meetings of teachers, parents, and others to provide information about the National Agenda. There is increasing awareness of the goals and an understanding of their importance in the education of students with visual impairments. The Kentucky School for the Blind (KSB) has been involved in a strategic planning process. As a result of focus groups held around the state, the Kentucky School for the Blind developed the following nine "Key Directions": regional program development, KSB/LEA collaboration, vision specific skills, public relations, enrollment, technology, residential programming, academic curriculum, and vocational programs. Each key direction has a committee charged with providing recommendations pertaining to the particular focus. Each committee chair has been provided with information regarding the National Agenda and asked to have the goals embedded within all recommendations. Kentuckians are continuing to examine their state's educational services to identify any gaps and will use the National Agenda Goal Statements as guides.

Maine—Reported by Jean T. Small. Teachers and education counselors from the State Division for the Blind and Visually Impaired are directing the National Agenda efforts in Maine. They have selected Goals 1, 4, 5, 6, and 7 as most in need of immediate attention. Action plans have been developed for each of these goals. For Goal 1, they are developing information packets to share with community resources and increasing personal contacts to expand their referral base. For Goal 4, all teachers serving visually impaired children have sent revised service plans indicating the instructional needs of students. The Division for the Blind

will be working with the legislature to provide adequate numbers of teachers to meet these needs. Goal 5 is being addressed by disseminating the OSEP policy statement on the low incidence of personnel preparation, with accompanying synopsis, to state and local education authorities and parents. (See Appendix G for the OSEP policy statements.) For Goal 6, a "screening system" is being developed to eliminate the need for teachers to see all referrals. A packet of information indicating assessments used in the program will be available for families and schools at the time of referral. This will be updated annually. Goal 7 is being addressed initially through a committee at the Instructional Materials Center (IMC) that will prioritize goals based on data obtained via a survey regarding the IMC. The remaining National Agenda goals will be addressed in the coming year.

Massachusetts—Reported by Karen Ross. Information packets containing the National Agenda booklet are routinely distributed to state legislators, Department of Education special services personnel, professionals, and parents. Presentations on the National Agenda and the core curriculum (Goal 8) have been made at state and regional conferences for professionals, parents, and families as well as in university graduate courses. A new organization of vision professionals—the Association of Massachusetts Educators of Students with Visual Impairments (AMESVI)—has established a subcommittee to conduct an extensive survey of certified vision teachers across the state. Data gathered will help in compiling demographics regarding caseloads, work environments, professional development needs, as well as instructional materials and adaptive equipment. A Braille Literacy Day was held at the State House in Boston. Speakers addressed the impact of the recently passed Braille Law on the education of students with visual impairments. Statewide implementation leaders for six of the National Agenda goals have been identified to date. Efforts are underway to reinstate the Massachusetts Federation of Agencies of and for the Blind as a vehicle for enhancing collaboration among the state's diverse organizations and independent service providers.

Michigan—Reported by Kathy Brown. Michigan has formed a steering committee to work on the National Agenda goals for Michigan. This committee, consisting of teachers, parents, O&M instructors, administrators, and university instructors, has representatives from MAER, CEC, the media center, the Commission for the Blind, and other agencies serving individuals who are visually impaired. Monthly meetings are held to discuss issues, strategies, and action plans. The steering committee has established subcommittees with additional participants from throughout the state. Each subcommittee addresses one specific goal and efforts are underway to determine strengths, weaknesses, and the steps needed to achieve each goal within Michigan.

Missouri—Reported by Jennie Mascheck. The Missouri School for the Blind (MSB) has assumed leadership in the statewide efforts toward a vision that parallels the National Agenda. MSB hosted a summit for education and rehabilitation professionals working with Missouri's children and youths who are visually impaired, including those with multiple disabilities. Participants were asked to identify: elements of service being done well; improvements needed; threats to improvement; opportunities currently available; additional resources necessary to successfully implement and deliver programs; and the level of quality of services. A variety of activities and projects, with statewide implications, was targeted for continuation or initiated as a result of the summit.

Family learning vacations and a parents' advisory council were established to promote parental involvement and provide family-focused services on behalf of visually impaired children aged birth through five years. INSITE, VIISA, Hand in Hand Training, and Weekends with the Experts are among the professional development activities sponsored by MSB. Recent efforts have proposed revisions to the state's competencies for teachers of students who are visually impaired and expansion of university course offerings for braille literacy. A work group is developing a proposal for a state information resources clearinghouse for professionals serving Missouri children who are visually impaired. An Educate America: Goals 2000 grant to modify curricula and instruction will address the core curriculum. Focus groups are soon to be formed to evaluate assessment and instruction. A survey mailed to fifty teachers certified in the education of students with visual impairments provided information about caseload sizes. This was shared with the National Goal Leader (NGL) for Goal 4.

New Hampshire—Reported by William A. Finn. The National Agenda goals are very much in agreement with long-standing educational philosophies, activities, and efforts in New Hampshire. Information packets and related materials about the National Agenda have been shared with parents, educators, legislators, policy makers, and a variety of other interested groups and individuals. The State Department of Education, university system, and other stakeholders work collaboratively on a Special Education Statewide Task Force. A significant effort has been made to revise certification standards for teachers of students with visual impairments. New Hampshire has also formed Inter-Agency Vision Support Seminars (IViSS), a multi-agency effort to provide in-service training related to the education and rehabilitation of individuals who are blind or visually impaired. To date, six seminars have been held. Interagency collaboration has been strengthened in support of consumer groups such as the NH chapter of the National Association for Parents of the Visually Impaired (NAPVI), and the National Association for Albinism and Hypopigmentation (NOAH) has been established.

New Mexico—Reported by Donna Stryker. New Mexico's efforts have focused on four major areas: information dissemination, informal decision making, training, and formation of a National Agenda steering committee. National Agenda information packets have been distributed at state AER meetings and mailed to legislators, policy makers, and local special education administrators. In addition, presentations about the National Agenda have been made to parent, professional, and consumer organizations. Presently, there is an insufficient number of teachers in New Mexico specially trained to meet the core curricular needs of students with visual impairments. This problem is exacerbated because no visual disability-specific teacher training program exists in our state university system. Currently, three basic courses are taken by teachers in the state. Three additional courses are expected to be offered.

New York—Reported by Emily Leyenberger and Victoria Tripodi. Most activities have been in the areas of information sharing and dissemination. Information has been shared and discussed with New York State officials such as the Director of Special Education and other policy makers. Presentations have been made at NYSAER, to urban school district teachers and administrators, and to families of children who are blind or visually impaired. An article was published in a state-wide newsletter for schools for the blind. Letters were sent to offices of the State Commission for the Blind encouraging responses to Goal 6 (assessment) data-collection questionnaires.

Plans are underway to establish an action-oriented committee charged with developing a New York State Agenda based on the National Agenda model. The New York Institute for Special Education has implemented activities specific to the core curriculum (Goal 8) areas of career education, technology, and social integration. In career education, the goal is to enhance career choices in a supportive environment and provide an inclusionary program fostering cooperation and communication between schools and community businesses. The program includes training and job experiences in a variety of jobs both on and off campus. In technology, students are introduced to computers equipped with speech synthesizers and screen-access software. Students with low vision have access to font-enhancing software and low vision evaluations to complement educational plans designed to maximize use of residual vision. Social integration with nondisabled peers is provided across many disciplines—for example, academics, athletics, recreation, and vocational education.

North Carolina—Reported by George Lee.
North Carolina is addressing Goal 3, personnel preparation, through efforts to establish a teacher training program at North Carolina Central University in Durham. Additional efforts are underway with Goal 8, core curriculum, encouraging local schools to recognize the importance of both the core curriculum and parent education.

Ohio—Reported by Marjorie Ward.
Ohio has formed subcommittees in response to challenges inherent in the eight goals of the National Agenda. Representatives from public residential and local school programs, parent organizations, medical and public health agencies, special education regional resource centers, and early childhood programs attended a meeting to determine how Ohio might address the National Agenda. Those in attendance volunteered to either chair or serve on one of the eight goal-related subcommittees. Each chair has worked with their subcommittee to de-

velop a plan of action addressing their specific goal and first steps have been taken toward implementation.

Oklahoma—Reported by Robert Warren.
The Oklahoma School for the Blind (Parkview) has been actively disseminating information and otherwise promoting the National Agenda. Presentations have been made at statewide meetings of parents, educators, and consumers. Parkview School's Advisory Committee developed a statewide strategic plan addressing the educational needs of children in Oklahoma with visual impairments. Oklahoma's strategic plan contains most of the components of the National Agenda. State legislation directing a statewide task force to study the feasibility of producing textbooks in appropriate media has been implemented.

Oregon—Reported by Ann Hicks.
The Oregon School for the Blind in concert with the State Regional Management Team has endorsed the National Agenda. A working group, consisting of teachers of students with visual impairments from all regions of the state, has made specific recommendations for prioritizing the goals on which they will be focusing their efforts. Requests for information and surveys received from National Goal Leader (NGL) organizations have been responded to. A Joint Action Committee with representatives from education, university training, adult services, consumer groups, and parents has been formed. They will be working to help Oregon achieve the goals of the National Agenda. University partnerships are underway to provide teachers of students with visual impairments competencies in the area of orientation and mobility.

Pennsylvania—Reported by Diane P. Wormsley.
The Management Team of the Overbrook School for the Blind has examined what needs to be done to promote and implement the National Agenda throughout Pennsylvania. Cynthia Jackson-Glenn, a parent, has volunteered to co-chair this statewide effort. A presentation was given at the Pennsylvania Conference for Educators of Persons with Visual Impairment (PCEVI). Attendees were informed of the work done thus far and discussed ways to best proceed for its full implementation. Packets of information have been distributed widely to educators, parents, and consumers. A presentation on the National Agenda was also made at the Fourth International Con-

ference on Education and Rehabilitation of People with Disabilities in Korea. Graduate students in the Pennsylvania College of Optometry teacher preparation programs receive information about the National Agenda as part of their course work.

South Carolina—Reported by Lin Mackechnie and Suzanne Swaffield. South Carolina's statewide coordinators routinely distribute information about the National Agenda to professionals, parents, and related service providers throughout the state. Information packets have also been sent to all newly elected state legislators and members of the Ways and Means and Educational subcommittees. The National Agenda goals have been infused into the Statewide Training Initiative for Special Education Coordinators and Teachers and is part of the training for new special education coordinators and teachers of children with visual impairments. Presentations on the National Agenda were made at meetings of the South Carolina AER and at a parent training weekend sponsored by the School for the Deaf and the Blind. Further development of the South Carolina state plan, incorporating the National Agenda Goals, is underway.

Tennessee—Reported by Grace Ambrose. Efforts have focused on disseminating National Agenda public information packets to special education leaders in Nashville and elsewhere as well as to state legislators. Presentations made at various conferences of educators, parents, and consumers indicate much general agreement with the goals and process of the National Agenda.

Texas—Reported by Cyral Miller and Phil Hatlen. Texans have spent the past year spreading the word to related agencies and organizations and moving closer to meeting the Agenda's goals. Following are some of the active efforts addressing them. For Goal 2, parent involvement, steps have been taken to assure that all families, including Spanish-speaking and/or blind members, have information about visual impairment and available services. In the past year, a quarterly newsletter about visual impairment and deaf/blindness, jointly produced and distributed by the Texas School for the Blind (TSBVI) and the Texas Commission for the Blind, has been provided in Spanish, large print, braille, cassette, and electronically via the World Wide Web as well as in disk formats. A new networking effort is being launched at TSBVI specifically for Spanish-speaking families with visually impaired children.

For Goal 3, personnel preparation, university instructors, Regional Education Service Center consultants, parents, and staff of the Texas Education Agency and TSBVI are working to create a coordinated, accessible system of personnel preparation. A full-time coordinator is assigned to this project.

For Goal 4, caseload sizes, a committee is actively researching current caseloads of professionals teaching children with visual impairments throughout the state and hopes to have results available in the spring of 1998. A group of vision and O&M consultants from the Educational Regional Service Centers are working with TSBVI on Goal 6, assessments, and are developing a process and format to document on a regional basis the achievement of students who are visually impaired. A pilot study underway will establish current data on regional student performance levels in all areas of the core curriculum. The document is not designed to measure individual progress or lead to individual education plans but should provide a new level of needs assessment for designing regional and statewide programs.

The Texas Education Agency is working on Goal 7, instructional materials in appropriate media, to assure that all braille textbooks arrive at local schools at the same time as the books for print readers. Data will be collected on timeliness of delivery during the 1997–98 school year. Texas legislation mandates that textbook publishers provide accessible electronic files of their books to braille producers, which has proved to have a positive impact on the on-time delivery of braille textbooks.

Goal 8, core curriculum, is being addressed through the Outreach Department at TSBVI as they offer training for local districts on "Quality Programming for Visually Impaired Students" (QPVI) that stresses the core curriculum. Texas suggests that this be considered as a model for providing training related to the core curriculum for students who are visually impaired. Texas plans to continue these activities, as well as others, and to involve professionals, parents, and adults who are visually impaired in achieving all of the National Agenda goals.

Utah—Reported by Lee Robinson. A committee, co-chaired by a parent and the Superintendent of the Utah Schools for the Deaf and Blind, is facilitating Utah's activities related to the National Agenda. A specific committee is addressing Goal 7, availability of texts in accessible media. With support from teachers, parents, and consumers, a "braille bill" has been enacted by the state legislature. This provides appropriations for increased availability of braille textbooks, braille instruction, and other braille literacy projects throughout the state. Infants and children with visual impairments are placed within time lines specified in the state plan for implementation of IDEA. The average time between referral and service entry is thirty days for school-age children and forty-five days for infants. Other National Agenda goals receiving particular attention by the Utah committee include Goals 2 (parent involvement) and 3 (assessment).

Vermont—Reported by Stephanie Bissonette. Vermont has reviewed its status with regard to meeting each of the eight goals. The results are as follows. Goal 1 (early referral): students and their families are referred to an appropriate education program within thirty days of identification of a suspected visual impairment. Goal 2 (parent involvement): schools distribute a policies and procedures statement to ensure the rights of all parents to full participation and equal partnership in the education process. Although VABVI does not have a written policy, teachers do acknowledge the vital role of parents and assure that they have equal participation in educational planning. Goal 3 (personnel preparation): there is no university in Vermont preparing educators of students with visual impairments. Goal 4 (caseload sizes): Vermont states that "service providers will determine caseloads based on the needs of students and will require ongoing professional development for all teachers and O&M instructors." This is acknowledged to be a challenge because there are only five employed teachers to serve 215 students with visual impairments, fifty percent of whom have multiple disabilities. The caseload average is thirty-five students per teacher over a large geographic area. Goal 5 (placement options): as in many states, students do not have access to a full array of placement options within Vermont. Goal 6 (assessments): assessments are conducted in collaboration with parents by personnel with expertise in the education of students with visual impairments. Goal 7 (availability of texts in accessible media): access to developmental and educational services includes assurance that instructional materials are available in the appropriate media and at the same time as those for sighted peers. Each itinerant teacher has a laptop computer, with a Duxbury translator and a Braille Blazer (embosser). Numerous volunteer braille transcribers within the state assist in meeting this goal. Goal 8 (core curriculum): educational and developmental goals and instruction reflect the assessed needs of students in all academic areas and most of the disability-specific core curricula, such as O&M, social skills, recreation, career education, independent living skills, assistive technology, and visual efficiency skills. The biggest challenge in fully meeting this goal is finding time to address all areas of need. Of the five itinerant teachers, four are also O&M certified, but still have large caseloads.

Virginia—Reported by Barbara McCarthy. Presentations have been made at various state meetings and to the Virginia Department of Education's Special Education Advisory Committee. Packets of information about the National Agenda and core curriculum have also been distributed. A recommendation to develop a state plan, using the National Agenda as a guide, was presented to the Virginia Board of Education's Special Education Advisory Committee. It is anticipated that the recommendation will be approved and the development of a state plan will be underway.

West Virginia—Reported by Donna See. West Virginia has gathered data regarding the current status of each National Agenda goal. With the exception of Goal 3 (personnel preparation), these goal areas are addressed in state education policies. A higher education task force is working to have a certification program for teachers of children with visual impairments in the near future. For Goal 4 (caseload sizes), a statewide task force ensures that IEPs include time for curriculum and material modifications and adaptations. Also, an O&M task force determines "best practice" for students who are visually impaired. Detailed studies of the remaining goals are underway to determine if state policy is being implemented on local levels.

Wisconsin—Reported by Andrew Papineau. Wisconsin has been actively involved in the National Agenda process. A joint Department of Public Instruction and Wisconsin AER Committee has been formed to work on the eight goal statements. Committee members include teachers, administrators, and parents. One specific task is to address Goal 8, the core curriculum. A resource list of assessments and curricula currently used is being compiled. Additionally, curricula in use across the country have been ordered and will be reviewed with the aim of developing guidelines for teachers of students with visual impairments in Wisconsin.

The Superintendent of the Department of Public Instruction has been made aware of the National Agenda and has directed that an informational bulletin be developed to address specific needs of children with visual disabilities. This will be distributed along with the "Policy Guidance on Educating Blind and Visually Impaired Students" prepared by the U.S. Office of Special Education and Rehabilitative Services (see Appendix G).

Wyoming—Reported by Janet Wood. The National Agenda public information packets have been disseminated widely to parents, Protection & Advocacy, special education directors, and AER members throughout Wyoming. Subsequently, there has been an increased number of concerns voiced to the Department of Education regarding services for students with visual impairments. It may be assumed that parents are becoming more aware of appropriate programming through the information provided. The individual submitting this report states, "I believe that it [National Agenda packet] has been the impetus behind the complaints as well as the model for the responses to the complaints. In a state as rural as Wyoming, with the push for local control, and the small number of visually impaired students, I believe the National Agenda needs to move forward, literally one student at a time, and it is doing just that."

SUMMARY AND CONCLUSIONS

There are two primary questions that emerge from this first *Report to the Nation:* What have we learned from the data? How will the goals be achieved?

What Have We Learned from the Data?

This question must be divided into different components of the National Agenda effort. First, data from the NGL reports provide a snapshot of what the nation's educational services offer children and youths with visual impairments, including those with multiple disabilities. They provide information about the timely referrals of children to education services, how involved parents consider themselves to be in their children's education process, how many assessment instruments are used, and so forth. The second component described in this report relates to the level of activity within states as they seek to achieve the eight goals within their own state. And third, the listing of endorsing organizations and advisory boards, along with the National Goal Leaders, provides information representing the extent of involvement of schools, organizations, and individuals involved in the National Agenda.

Overall, the National Goal Leaders found that some processes are in place while others need stimulation, augmentation, and, in some cases, creation. It is important to note that the parents, teachers, and other professionals to whom surveys were predominantly distributed were already in systems that provided services. At a time when the nation is not producing a sufficient number of teachers or orientation and mobility instructors (Goal 3), it is difficult to locate and reach the fam-ilies whose children are not receiving education services from a qualified teacher or O&M instructor of students with visual impairments.

Based on the ages at which children were diagnosed and then referred to education services, the Foundation for Blind Children learned that referrals were not conducted within the thirty days of suspected visual impairment, as the goal requires. Efforts will need to be directed to the medical communities where this time lag can be reduced. The Foundation also learned that only half of the children were initially diagnosed with a visual impairment by ophthalmologists. This finding is particularly important because if educators want medical personnel to learn the importance of early specialized services, their efforts cannot be directed solely within the ophthalmological community.

For Goal 2, the National Association of Parents of the Visually Impaired (NAPVI) inquired about the extent to which parents were knowledgeable and comfortable with their involvement in the education process for their children. Although the parents who responded to the survey were already involved in a parents' organization or had attended a function sponsored by one of two special schools, it was interesting to see that levels of knowledge and comfort were not reflective of the extent to which IDEA provides for parent involvement. The data the NAPVI gathered also showed that more than one in four parents did not feel very knowledgeable (better than a midpoint rating on a five-point Likert-type scale) about the six areas about which they were asked (e.g., knowledge of their children's current abilities). With regard to their levels of comfort, the overall ratings were somewhat better. However, when one in four expressed that they were not comfortable (beyond the midpoint) in attending their children's IEP/IFSP meetings and that only 65 percent feel comfortable disagreeing with professionals concerning their children's programs, there is reason for concern. The information from this research effort may serve as a stimulus for education programs and parents to discuss whether stronger partnerships may be formed resulting in more knowledge and comfort on the part of parents. It is interesting to note that although parents indicated levels of knowledge and comfort that were not very high, 93 percent also responded that they considered themselves involved in their children's education.

The Division on Personnel Preparation (Division 17) of the Association for the Education and Rehabilitation of the Blind and Visually Impaired served as the National Goal Leader for Goal 3. They were interested in learning about the quantity of personnel available and becoming available to provide education and orientation and mobility services to children and youths with visual impairments, including those with multiple disabilities. Division 17 took a two-pronged approach to respond to the goal: (1) they looked at the numbers of children who would be in need of services and (2) they surveyed university programs to learn if a sufficient number of professionals were being prepared to serve the children. Division 17 found a great discrepancy between the numbers of children reported to have visual impairments and the numbers for whom the government plans to provide services. This difference was attributed to the ways in which children are counted. Their most startling findings were how few professionals are being prepared on a national basis. Without dramatic changes in the system for supplying a sufficient number of teachers and orientation and mobility instructors, achievement of the other goals may become moot. Children and youths with visual impairments may be referred for services, find braille materials available, have opportunities for their parents' involvement, and so forth. However, without the specially trained personnel to deliver the specialized instruction, an education cannot be fulfilled.

Goal 4 deals with the sizes of caseloads of teachers and the provision of continuing education for professionals supplying direct service. For this goal the Association of State Educational Consultants for the Visually Impaired (ASECVI) provided the national picture. They solicited and compiled specific state policies regarding caseloads and determined that size of caseloads should be individually determined. They furnished us with state-specific guidelines and through case studies exemplify the rationale for the recommendation. These case studies illustrate the complexities and challenges facing professionals whose jobs are to provide education services. They detail information about which states specify numerical limits for caseloads. They offer questions to assist school districts in developing caseload policies and describe how individual states have caseload management systems in place. Flexibility and individualization for states and school districts are presented as important to allow for adjustments to the needs of individual caseloads.

The Council of Schools for the Blind (COSB) gathered data to determine the extent to which parents were provided with information about access to a full array of services available for their children. Among their findings, only 28.1 percent of 359 parents indicated that various placement options were explained to them during their children's IEP meetings and nearly half of these parents indicated that only two options were presented. One of COSB's conclusions is that "parents are not given the information they need to truly participate." Because the COSB survey represents parents whose children are already in programs, caution must be used when generalizing from these data. It may be that parents of children without services are not provided with any information about local services or other options. The situation may also be reviewed every year. Nonetheless, COSB has supplied clear evidence that school systems are not, to a great extent, providing the information required by IDEA and reaffirmed through OSEP's Policy Guidance Statement (see Appendix G).

Assessment of a student's present levels of functioning is a cornerstone to providing an appropriate education. The Lighthouse, Inc. gathered information including but not limited to: assessments used, which professionals administered assessment instruments, and the extent to which parents were involved in the assessment processes and their interpretation. Through surveys, they learned that many instruments were employed throughout the country. They expressed concern that these instruments were often locally modified when they were not designed to be used with a population of children with visual impairments. There were no established protocols so that children with visual disabilities would be assessed in specific areas of development, achievement, or disability-specific skills. Further, discrepancies were found between parent and professional reports of the extent to which parents are truly involved in the assessment procedures. Although these findings are a national snapshot and it is known that in some areas of the country appropriate and comprehensive assessment are being conducted, it is gratifying to know that through such efforts their findings may stimulate projects of national significance to assist local teachers, orientation and mobility instructors, psychologists, and diagnosticians in evaluating instruments currently used, establishing guidelines for protocols and instrument modifications, creating training opportunities for those providing assessments, and so forth.

The extent to which developmental and instructional materials for children with visual impairments were available and provided in a timely way was the focus of a survey conducted by the Association of Instructional Resource Centers for the Visually Handicapped (AIRCVH). They analyzed data from twenty-seven states serving 25,000 students. They found that, on average, materials ordered in May were received within four-and-one-half to five weeks, those ordered in July took six-and-one-half to seven weeks, and those ordered in September would take six-and-one-half to seven weeks; by September 15, fourteen states (52 percent) stated that between 81 and 100 percent of their students were still awaiting ordered materials. While it is understood that some students might move during the summer months, it is clear that many students could not expect to have their books and other specialized developmental or instructional materials at the beginning of the school year when their sighted classmates received theirs. AIRCVH also provided information about which states offer learning media assessments, clinical low vision evaluations for optical devices, and so forth. These data present the differences in services that families might expect from one state to another. Therefore, what might be considered "best practices" for students with visual impairments may not be available in a uniform manner.

Early referrals for education services, parent involvement, a sufficient number of teachers, realistic caseloads, appropriate assessments, a full array of service delivery options, and available materials will not in themselves provide an appropriate education. The last, but certainly not the least important goal—the provision of a core curriculum for students with visual impairments—is necessary so that children and youths may benefit from the other goals. As recommended by the participants in the 1995 Josephine L. Taylor Leadership Institute, the Texas School for the Blind and Visually Impaired defined, developed, and disseminated the disability-specific core curriculum for students with visual impairments, including those with multiple disabilities. Annotated bibliographical information was also prepared related to the core areas addressed by the curriculum. Currently, TSBVI is working to obtain endorsements of the core curriculum. A small sample survey was also conducted of teachers of students with visual impairments to ascertain their acceptance of this curriculum, and one of the questions involved possible barriers to its implementation. Responses included several of the topics addressed by previous goals of the National Agenda (e.g., caseload size and inadequate assessment materials). Additional barriers include such areas as support from school administrators and providing time in a student's schedule. However, the response that teachers of students with visual impairments are expected to cover academic work is of greatest concern. In 1984, and again in 1991, the Division of Visual Impairments of the Council for Exceptional Children adopted a position paper on the roles and functions of such teachers. It seems clear that this professional group does not consider "tutoring" an accepted role. Although teaching core curricular subjects within academics is clearly appropriate, such as teaching the use of a magnifier to read a map, academic subjects need to be a part of the regular education program, thus allowing more time for the core curriculum.

This summary of the data generated by the National Goal Leaders provides only a portion of their overall findings. Their reports are rich with information and compel everyone working toward achievement of the National Agenda goals to set quantitative levels for attainment. The snapshot they present confirms the beliefs of the original more than five hundred people who established the National Agenda: that all was not right with the education services provided to the nation's children and youths with visual impairments.

Nonetheless, these data are also promising. Parents were found who felt knowledgeable about their children's education needs, a portion of braille and large-print books were being delivered in a timely manner, and comprehensive assessments were available in some locations. All in all, this snapshot also shows what "can be" and for some students "what is." Knowing that the goals reflect the needs, and that some children and youths receive what should be available for all and so many parents and professionals are committed to working toward reaching the National Agenda goals, provides a hope that, by the next *Report to the Nation,* data will reflect true progress.

How Will the Goals be Achieved?

The National Agenda was established as a grassroots effort. Achievement of each goal, and the agenda as a whole, will come about from a grassroots effort as well, which may mean a local teacher and parents advocating for students to receive a sufficient amount of services in response to their assessed needs. It may mean groups of professionals in a school district working for change in the procedures of that district or it may be parents, meeting at a national conference, to discuss how individual parents can advocate for their child to receive the core curriculum in a local or special school. And it may be an adult with a visual impairment volunteering time with a teenager who is blind to learn from an "expert" how to implement lessons from the core curriculum in the community.

Beginning with advocacy for individual children, and reaching out to ensure that appropriate procedures are in place, the goals will be achieved. Likewise, in order to ensure that the goals can be achieved for individual children, the appropriate supports must be in place at state and national levels. For example, production of braille books must use state-of-the art technology in state and national production facilities so that they will reach local districts and ultimately individual students when they are needed.

The grassroots approach involves the ability of individuals, as well as groups of parents, professionals, and persons with visual impairments, to make change at all levels of education services for children and youths with visual impairments. As stated earlier, these changes are brought about by personal and group initiatives. Parents, professionals, and persons with visual impairments must be the ones to assess, initiate, and implement the changes—and ultimately be responsible for achieving the eight goals of the National Agenda.

Prior to publication of the National Agenda booklet, meetings were held during a JLTLI to develop strategies for local and regional efforts for achieving the National Agenda. These strategies were included in the National Agenda booklet and many education programs are already finding them appropriate and effective for their delivery of services. Although the eight goals represent a non-exhaustive list of "goals" for children and youths with visual impairments, the eight goals will, from now until the year 2000, receive special attention.

For individual children, advocacy may include the question, "Did John receive his books in braille at the same time as his sighted classmates?" If not, "What steps were taken to ensure that he will receive all educational materials throughout the rest of the year at the same time as his classmates?" Another question might be, "Did Tasha receive the orientation and mobility services to improve her use of distance vision as was indicated on her functional vision assessment?" If not, "What steps were taken to ensure that she receives this subject in the Core Curriculum for Students with Visual Disabilities in a timely manner?" "Are there sufficient numbers of O&M specialists being trained to meet the needs?"

At the endorsing schools and organizations, commitment to achieve the National Agenda may take place through tasks related to improving their service delivery for each of the National Agenda's goals. For example, in a school district that has endorsed the National Agenda, there may be a self-study of the level to which parents consider themselves full participants in their children's educational planning. Steps may be taken to address the concerns of parents who do not as yet consider themselves full participants. At a university that prepares teachers of students with visual impairments, which has also endorsed the National Agenda, there may be a new initiative to work with a neighboring state department of education to establish a three-year plan to supply a "sufficient number of teachers" to address shortages within the state.

States, through the work of their National Agenda coordinators and various committees, are addressing the goals in various ways. As shown in the state reports, some states have selected specific goals as their focus while others have elected to work on all eight goals. Still others have adapted goals to meet specific priorities within their state. Each state's coordinators have helped the parents, professionals, and persons with visual impairments to ascertain in what ways the national goals relate to the status of services within their state. Although achievement of all goals in the nation will depend on the extent to which all geographical areas are able to reach those goals, the freedom to make the National Agenda "their own state agenda" has helped to gain support and commitment for effecting positive change for children and youths with visual impairments.

At the national level, the advisory board and the co-chairs are functioning as resources and guides to help in achieving the goals. From providing presentations at state, regional, or national conferences to developing National Agenda packets of information for distribution, the national efforts to achieve the goals provide support, organization, technical assistance, and publications to parents, professionals, and persons with visual impairments who are working to achieve the goals.

How Are the Goals Related to Each Other?

The eight goals of the National Agenda were identified as having the highest impact on the education of children and youths with visual impairments as well as the highest likelihood of achievement by the year 2000. The question remains whether these goals are related to each other or if they work in concert toward achieving real change. At first glance, they appear to cover broad topics, from the preparation of a sufficient number of teachers to the provision of educational materials, from parent involvement in education

planning to determining caseload sizes for teachers and orientation and mobility instructors. Nonetheless, although some relate to administrative changes and others are concerned with direct service with children and youths, a relationship does exist among the goals. As first offered in the National Agenda document,

IF

- there is an adequate supply of well-prepared teachers [Goal 3], who benefit from early referrals [Goal 1], and from having parents as partners [Goal 2], and have manageable caseloads [Goal 4];
- a full array of placement options are available [Goal 5];
- children's placements are based on quality assessments [Goal 6];
- instructional materials are available in the right media at the right time [Goal 7]; and
- a disability-specific core curriculum is implemented for all visually impaired students [Goal 8];

THEN

educators will have entered the 21st century assured of having the tools to prepare children with visual impairments for a fulfilling and satisfying adult life.

There is also an architectural infrastructure when two or more of the goals are examined together. For example, Goals 3 and 8 relate to each other. In the preparation of teachers, the core curriculum is essential in course work and practicum experiences; qualified teachers must be able to teach the disability-specific skills to children with varying characteristics. Although Goal 3 speaks directly to the need of a sufficient number of teachers, for each child to receive the core curriculum, there must be enough teachers available to provide the quality and quantity of services called for in Goal 8. In a similar way, Goals 1 and 5 are related. When medical personnel refer children within a timely manner to educational services, a teacher ready to accept immediate referrals is a necessity. If caseloads are so high that timely assessment and service delivery cannot be implemented, then an early referral becomes meaningless. For a last example, we see the relationship of Goals 6 and 7. Without appropriate materials for literacy or instruction to facilitate development, assessments cannot be appropriate. However, without qualified personnel to assess the children, having such materials will become meaningless.

In the Foreword to the *National Agenda for the Education of Children and Youths with Visual Impairments Including Those with Multiple Disabilities,* Judith Heumann, Assistant Secretary for the U.S. Department of Education, Office of Special Education and Rehabilitative Services, wrote:

> Each of these eight goals, these signposts and watchwords of wisdom, is a broad brush stroke that will form for us a picture of equality and opportunity. Taken together, they paint a picture of the future, a future based on increased positive outcomes (p. vi).

DETAILED STATE INFORMATION ON CLASS SIZE CASELOAD COMPOSITION

Submitted by the Association of State Educational Consultants for the Visually Impaired
Prepared by Sharon Knoth

ALABAMA

290-080-09-.18   Caseload

All caseloads except multiple disabilities, mentally retarded (IQ of below thirty and concurrent deficits in adaptive behavior), and autism can be increased by twenty-five percent with the addition of one full-time paraprofessional. The following numbers are to be utilized when determining appropriate caseloads for teachers who provide special education services to exceptional students ages six to twenty-one.

Exceptionality	Elementary		Middle		High	
	1*–6†		7*–8†		9*–12†	
Deaf-Blind	5	10	5	10	5	10
Visually Impaired	10	15	10	15	10	15
Multiple Disabilities	All special education teachers assigned to this exceptionality may serve no more than four total students. This teacher, with a paraprofessional, may serve eight total students, up to a maximum of two paraprofessionals serving twelve total students.					

*Maximum number of students at any one time.
†Total number of students.

ARIZONA

Arizona's Department of Education has a booklet entitled *Enhancing Students with Visual Impairments in Arizona* that was developed by the Sensory Impairment Advisory Committee. This booklet states:

> The following ranges for class size and caseloads are based on state and national averages for agencies to use as a **general guide** in establishing local caseloads and class sizes. These ranges should **not** be viewed as established minimum state requirements.

Type of Program	Class Size and Caseload Ranges
Resource room (one teacher and one aide)	8 to 12 students
Self-contained classrooms (one teacher and one aide):	
Preschool	4 to 8 students
Kindergarten through third grade	6 to 8 students
Fourth through twelfth grade	8 to 10 students
Multihandicapped	3 to 7 students
Itinerant services:	
Itinerant teacher*	6 to 12 students
Orientation and mobility instructor	8 to 12 students
Home-based instructor (preschool age)	13 to 17 students

*The number of students on an itinerant teacher's average caseload will be affected by the number of braille students served by that teacher and by the travel time required. The itinerant teacher will, on average, provide twenty hours per week of direct services to students.

ARKANSAS

1993 Guidelines

Maximum Teacher/Pupil Ratio Chart (based on full-time equivalency)

	Indirect Services	Itinerant Instruction	Resource Services	Special Class Services Options		
Noncategorical	1:40	1:35	1:25	1:15	1:10	1:6
Categorical	1:40	1:25	1:25	1:15	1:10	1:6
Visual Impairment		1:20	1:15			

When calculating the number of students being served, each student is counted one time. The following represents exceptions to the stated maximum teacher/pupil ratios:

1. For each student receiving special class services within a resource setting, not to exceed a total of three students, the maximum teacher/pupil ratio will be reduced by one student.
2. For each student receiving braille instruction from an itinerant instructor, the maximum teacher/pupil ratio will be reduced by two students.

Waiver from the Maximum Teacher/Pupil Ratio: Caseload

1. Should an emergency situation arise creating the need to request a waiver from the maximum teacher/pupil ratio, the public agency must submit a letter to its Special Education Area Supervisor stating the reason(s) for exceeding the maximum teacher/pupil ratio and outlining a plan to correct the problem. The Area Supervisor will respond in writing either approving or disapproving the variance.
2. A ten-percent variance (upward caseload adjustment) of the maximum teacher/pupil ratio is the maximum variance approvable before funding is affected. For example, the noncategorical resource setting teacher/pupil ratio is 1:25 with a ten percent variance equal to 2.5. When approved, this teacher/pupil ratio may then increase to 1:28. For a special class setting with a maximum teacher/pupil ratio of 1:15, a ten percent variance equals 1.5. When approved, the teacher/pupil ratio may increase to 1:17.
3. Prior to approval of the ten percent variance, a full-time paraprofessional must be employed for that class by the requesting district. For a 1:6 special class setting, a full-time paraprofessional is already required; therefore, an additional paraprofessional must be employed before a district's waiver will be approved.

Teacher/Pupil Ratio: Per Period Class Size

For itinerant instruction (excluding speech therapy) and resource services, a maximum of five students per period is the guideline. Where scheduling does not permit an even flow of five students per period, the number served should be as near to five as possible. Districts will not be cited for noncompliance with state standards when the per period class is eight students without a paraprofessional. However, the adopted guideline of five students per period is considered to be best educational practice and should be adhered to whenever possible. Exceptions to the adopted guideline of five students are:

1. When the special education teacher teaches one class per day in the area of personal/social adjustment as a pre-vocational or vocational class, the per period load may be adjusted upward not to exceed the maximum caseload.
2. When the teacher has a paraprofessional to assist in follow-through activities, the per period load may be adjusted upward not to exceed forty percent of the teacher/pupil ratio listed on the Maximum Teacher/Pupil Ratio Chart contained in this document.

CALIFORNIA

California Education Code and regulations do not dictate specific numbers or ranges for class size or caseload for staff serving visually impaired students. The only specific number for any caseload is twenty-eight for a Resource Specialist, who serves students with less severe disabilities at each school site. There is no differentiation between public school and residential programs. California is currently revising its funding model, service delivery system, and accountability standards. The proposed *DRAFT Guidelines for Students Who Are Visually Impaired* reads as follows:

It is recommended that programs use one or both of the following options in determining class sizes and caseloads:

Option I. Developing a process for establishing and monitoring the class size or a caseload of the teacher of the visually impaired or of the orientation and mobility specialist, based on the time required for:

Providing instruction based on the severity or intensity of student' needs
Consulting with medical personnel and community resource
Consulting and assisting parents
Traveling as necessary to carry out the responsibilities
Securing and preparing needed specialized materials, media, and equipment
Attending meetings, preparing reports, and record keeping
Include in the process ongoing communication between the staff member and the responsible supervisor or administrator to ensure that students are receiving appropriate instruction and services in accordance with the IEP and the changing needs of students.

Option II. Establish local caseloads and class sizes based on the age and the severity of needs of the students being served and the instruction and services needed to meet these needs.

The following ranges for class sizes and caseloads are based on state and national averages for agencies to use as a general guide in establishing local caseloads and class sizes. These ranges should not be viewed as establishing minimum state requirements.

Type of Program	Class Size and Caseload Ranges
Resource room (one teacher and one aide)	8 to 12 students
Self-contained classrooms (one teacher and one aide):	
Infants or preschool	4 to 8 students
Kindergarten through third grade	6 to 10 students
Fourth through twelfth grade	8 to 12 students
Multiple disabilities	3 to 7 students
Itinerant teacher	8 to 12 students
Orientation and mobility instructor	8 to 12 students
Home-based instructor (preschool age)	13 to 17 students

Local caseloads and class sizes of staff may fall above or below these ranges according to the time requirements outlined in Option I.

COLORADO

This is from a summary of the work of the Resource Allocation Committee.

Introduction to Caseload Management Guidelines

The Resource Allocation Committee's intent is to have guidelines for vision teachers that are "user friendly" and are specifically targeted to the needs of each district or service unit. Each student's needs would be evaluated and given a rating. The district or unit vision teacher would total the hours of service that all students require. Then they would add the minutes of travel time between destinations. Finally, a percentage of the work week to meet other duties involved in operating a program for vision services would be determined.

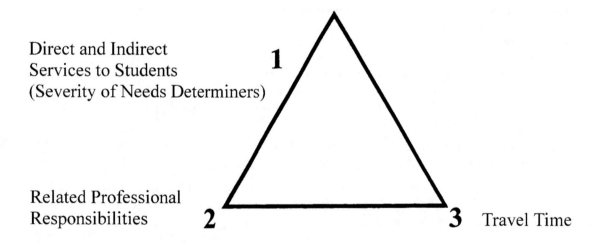

These three components combined determine caseload management. The following steps will help you:

Determine your present caseload
Check whether your caseload matches your designated contract hours

Step 1: Begin by determining the individual rating for each child who is identified with a visual impairment based on the severity of needs determiners (Severity Rating Scale).
Step 2: Total the number of hours of direct and indirect services to all students.
Step 3: Add to this the total travel (minutes *not* miles)

Step 4:   Then consider the amount of time necessary to meet related professional responsibilities such as those listed below:

- parent contact
- supervision of support staff
- in-services (preparation/presentations for staff, community, etc.)
- consultation with staff and administrators
- other district-assigned duties

- referral assessments
- writing reports
- materials preparation
- orders/materials inventory management
- professional development meetings (general education, teams, vision—local, regional, state)

Note: This component (Step 4) will vary to some extent based on individual programs. An average range for vision service providers is 25 percent to 40 percent of the week.

Step 5:   Total the hours of the three components. This gives you your total hours per week. Compare this with your contracted hours per week. These two numbers should match.

- If they do not match, does a paraprofessional or other support staff account for the difference?
- If they do not match and support staff does not account for the difference, the caseload should be re-evaluated.

SEVERITY RATING SCALE
FOR STUDENTS WITH VISUAL IMPAIRMENTS

Medical Evaluation

0   Normal visual acuity with full visual field, no significant pathology
1   Possible progressive disease, but one eye still within normal limits; mild nystagmus; bilateral strabismus that cannot be corrected; pre/post eye surgery; other severe temporary eye surgery; other severe temporary eye treatment, such as patching; significant bilateral field loss
2   Student with multiple impairments; cortical visual impairment; functionally visually impaired; delays in visual maturation
3   Acuity 20/70 to 20/200 in better eye after correction; a visual field of more than twenty degrees
4   Acuity of 20/200 to object perception in better eye after correction; a visual field of twenty degrees or less
5   Object perception to total blindness; a visual field of ten degrees or less

Reading Medium

0   Regular print with no modification; multi-impaired, nonreader; pre-reader
1   Regular print with magnification in addition to correction
2   Regular print with consistent use of magnification in addition to correction and/or large print
3   Technology for low vision; tape
4   Braille or pre-braille
5   Technology for braille

Compensatory Skill Needs/Adaptive or Developmental Training

0   Needs no compensatory skill instruction
1   Needs compensatory skill instruction in handwriting, fine and gross motor areas, and/or PE/recreational activities
2   Needs compensatory skill instruction in use of functional vision, sensory awareness, pre-vocational skills, use of low technology/adaptive equipment, and/or orientation to specific location
3   Needs compensatory skill instruction in concept development, use of basic low vision devices, computer/typing, map reading, geographical concepts and/or science concepts; career and vocational training; beginning O&M training

4   (In addition to #3) Needs compensatory skill instruction in tactual development, braille, abacus, slate and stylus, use of advanced low vision devices, daily living skills, advanced O&M training; vocational support

5   Needs advanced travel/cane skills; advanced math and science; transition between levels and placements; college preparation

Environmental Instructional Adjustments

0   Needs no adaptations of instructional materials or presentations

1   Needs some adapted written materials; dark copies; special seating; some magnification; extra lighting; materials storage area, and/or work area for special equipment

2   Needs occasional use of tapes; some adaptation of maps/graphs; frequent magnification, and/or extra lighting; requires some production of braille materials

3   Needs individually developed multisensory materials and adaptation; adaptive equipment such as switches and communication boards

4   Needs tapes; enlargement or adaptation of all instructional materials

5   Needs major production of braille; tactual adaptation of instructional materials; requires modified assignments, procedures and/or curriculum

Affective and Independent Behavior

Note: Severe emotional/social/behavioral needs rely on partnerships with other professionals in conjunction with the vision service provider. The following reflects the responsibilities of the vision service provider.

0   Needs no assistance in completing all assignments; involved in age-appropriate activities and adult/peer interactions; understands and positively accepts visual impairment; accesses own resources (role models, organization, etc.); is self advocate; multiply impaired, nonacademic; pre-academic

1   Needs minimal assistance with completing assignments and ordering materials (other than CIMC); requires encouragement for self advocacy; support for developing friendship; needs help understanding and explaining vision

2   Needs monitoring to complete assignments and ordering materials; requires assistance coping with visual impairments; difficulty initiating and maintaining friendships

3   Needs direct intervention for completing assignments and ordering materials; does not initiate or maintain friendship; denies visual impairment and/or its implications

Rating Scale Guidelines

  0–4   No Service

  5–9   Consult Service Only (one-half hour per month–one-half hour per week)

10–14   Light Service (one-half hour per week–five hours per week)

15–19   Moderate Service (five hours per week–twenty hours per week)

20–23   Heavy Service (more than twenty hours per week)

CONNECTICUT

Connecticut does not have guidelines or regulations regarding class size or caseload.

DELAWARE

The state is currently working on development of guidelines (regulations) for determining minimum level of itinerant service. Current caseloads are as follows:

Resource Room	1– 8	Legally blind students with a paraprofessional
	1–10	Partially sighted students with paraprofessional
Itinerant	1–25	Students

Resource room caseloads are determined by county; itinerant caseloads are determined geographically. The geographic determination is occasionally bypassed if there is a particular need on the part of the student, a teacher with a particular skill, or an imbalance in caseloads.

FLORIDA

All caseload determinations are completely locally based decisions. There are no state regulations regarding this issue.

GEORGIA

Class Sizes and Caseload

Program Area	Delivery Self-contained (SC) Resource (R)	Maximum W/O Para	Class Size With Para	Caseload
Visual impairment	SC	N/A	6	7
	R	3	4	13
Deaf-blind	SC	N/A	6	7

Note: Each paraprofessional (para) is equivalent to one-third teacher and affects individual class size and system average proportionately. Three paraprofessionals are the maximum number that can be used to reduce the maximum class size for any special education class.

If students from different programs are within the same segment, the class size is determined by the program with the smallest class size. The caseloads are determined by averaging the respective caseloads.

HAWAII

Hawaii does not have any class size or caseload regulations or recommendations. Students with visual impairments are primarily served on an itinerant basis. Most students with a visual impairment who also have multiple impairments attend the State School for the Visually and Hearing Impaired.

IDAHO

Idaho has standards for class sizes in the public school setting; however, they are not transferable to special education *per se*. Here is an example of part of their standards:

> The total number of students instructed by any one teacher for one week **shall** not exceed 160 per day calculated according to: The total number of students met per week divided by 5 **shall** not exceed 160 students daily. . . .

> The teacher's daily teacher assignment **shall** not exceed six hours. . . .

ILLINOIS

23 Illinois Administrative Code, Ch. I, S. 226.225, Subtitle A, Subchapter f reads as follows:

Section 226.225 Instructional Programs Class Size

The principal determinants of the number of students served in each special education instructional program shall be the age of the students, the nature and severity of their exceptional characteristics, and the degree of intervention necessary. All exceptions to the following program size limitations shall require the written approval of the State Board of Education prior to the implementation of the program.

a) Early childhood instructional programs shall have a maximum ratio of one (1) qualified teacher to five (5) students in attendance at any one given time; total enrollment shall be limited according to the needs of the students for individualized programming.

c) Instructional programs which primarily serve children whose principal exceptional characteristics are severe visual, auditory, physical, speech or language impairments, or behavioral disorders shall have maximum enrollment of eight (8) students.

e) Instructional programs which primarily serve children whose principal exceptional characteristics are moderate visual or auditory impairment shall have a maximum enrollment of twelve (12) students.

g) The local school district may increase the enrollment in a special education instructional program by a maximum of two (2) additional students to meet unique circumstances which occur during the school year. Such additions may be made only when the educational needs of all students who would be enrolled in the expanded program can be adequately and appropriately met, OR, the school district may increase the enrollment in a special education instructional program by a maximum of five (5) additional students when the program is provided with a full-time, non-certified assistant.

h) When the district wishes to exceed the maximum enrollments indicated above, approval shall be requested by writing to the State Board of Education, Department of Specialized Educational Services. The request shall include a rationale for the proposed enrollment variation and a plan for its evaluation. If the request for an enrollment deviation is denied, the district may appeal the decision to the State Superintendent of Education.

Section 226.240   Special Education Resource Programs

b) . . . Such instruction may be delivered in resource room classes or on an itinerant basis.

2) Enrollment in such a program shall be limited to the number of students who can effectively and appropriately receive assistance, ordinarily not to exceed a total of twenty (20). The teacher of each resource program shall actively participate in determining the appropriate enrollment.

INDIANA

Caseloads are addressed through the Indiana Administrative Code (IAC). There is nothing specific to the exceptionality of visual impairment and blindness.

511 IAC 7-3-8   Caseload
"Caseload" means the total number of students properly assigned to a special education teacher, speech-language pathologist, or a related services provider, and is generally determined by the number of individualized education programs for which that person has partial or entire implementation responsibility.

511 IAC 7-13-1(f)   An early childhood special education class cannot exceed eight students. At least one full-time instructional or program assistant is required to be assigned to the classroom in addition to the teacher.

511 IAC 7-13-1(g)   The caseload for a teacher providing consultation or home-based instruction for early childhood special education cannot exceed twenty students.

511 IAC 7-14-1(e)   The number of special education students assigned to a special education teacher, speech-language pathologist, or related services personnel is determined by:

    (1)   The nature and severity of the students' disabilities.
    (2)   The type and intensity of services needed as specified in the IEP.
    (3)   The chronological ages of the students.
    (4)   The chronological and mental age range of the students in part-time and full-time special education placements.

511 IAC 7-14-1(f)   The special education caseload shall be prorated and reduced as necessary if one (1) of the following circumstances exist:

    (1)   A full-time special education teacher or speech-language pathologist provides services to students in more than one of the placement options.
    (2)   The special education teacher or speech-language pathologist is employed or contracted on less than a full-time basis.
    (3)   The special education teacher or speech-language pathologist serves more than one building and travel is required.

Excluding early childhood, the law basically means that so long as the teacher is able to implement the IEPs of the students assigned to him or her, then the caseload is not too large. Once the teacher is no longer able to implement the IEPs as written, then the caseload must be reduced.

IOWA

Class sizes are addressed through the Administrative Rules of Special Education that provide limits for class sizes of certain service delivery models. Educational agencies are not limited to using any of these models:

Resource teaching program is an educational program for individuals who are enrolled in the general education curriculum for a majority of the school day but who require specially designed instruction in specific skill areas on a part-time basis . . . for a minimal average of thirty minutes per day. The maximum class size for this program is eighteen students . . . with the exception of programs for individuals with hearing impairment or visual impairment which shall have fifteen students.

Special class w/integration is an educational program for individuals who have similar educational needs and who can benefit from participation in the general academic offerings of the general education curriculum. The maximum class size for this program is twelve students at the elementary level and fifteen students at the secondary level with the exception of programs for hearing impairment or visual impairment which shall have ten students at both levels.

Self-contained special class w/little integration is an education program for individuals with similar educational needs who require specially designed instruction for most of their educational program but can benefit from limited participation in the general education curriculum with non-disabled individuals. The maximum class size for this program is eight students at the elementary level and ten students at the secondary level. The maximum class size of this program may be fifteen students if an AEA work experience coordinator coordinates and supervises off-campus work experience.

Self-contained special class is an educational program for individuals with severe disabilities who have similar educational needs and whose total instructional program must be specially designed and provided by a special education teacher. . . . The staff-to-students ratio for this program shall be one teacher and one educational aide for each group of five students. When students number six through nine are added, an additional educational aide must be employed. When the tenth student is added, another special education teacher must be employed.

The rules do not specify caseload sizes for itinerant teachers.

KANSAS

State regulations have various class size/caseload ranges depending on exceptionality area and type of services being provided.

Class Size and Caseload for a Center-based Program

Professional	Paraprofessionals Class Size	Maximum Disabled	Maximum Caseload
Integrated Classroom			
1 ECSE	1	12 (5 disabled)	10
1 ECSE	2	12 (8 disabled)	16
1 ECSE and 1 SE Team	2	18 (12 disabled)	24
Special Classroom			
1 ECSE	0	4	8
1 ECSE	1	8	16
1 ECSR and 1 SE Team	1	12	24

(continued)

Class Size and Caseload for a Center-based Program (*continued*)

Professional	Paraprofessionals Class Size	Maximum Disabled	Maximum Caseload
Home-Based Programs			
	1	0	16
	1	1	20
	1	2	24
	1	3	28

Class Size and Caseload for Programs for Severely Multiply Handicapped and Deaf-Blind

Program Level	Administrative Plan	Maximum Class Size and Caseload
All Levels	Special Classroom	2—with one or more paraprofessionals to a maximum of 4 students 5—with two or more paraprofessionals to a maximum of 8 students

KENTUCKY

707 KAR 1:230 Section 5 addresses caseload and class size. It reads:

1. Each LEA shall establish criteria in policies and procedures for caseloads for teachers of exceptional children. Caseloads for each teacher of exceptional children shall facilitate children and youth with disabilities attaining goals and outcomes required in KRS 158.6451 through the mastery of IEP goals and objectives.
2. Each LEA shall operate special education classes according to membership and age requirements for each disability and class plan as follows.

Disability and Class Plan	Maximum Membership and Total Age Range		Number and Age Range/Period	
Visual Disability				
Special class	10	6 years	N/A	N/A
Resource class	10	6 years	7	4 years
Itinerant teacher	12	N/A	7	4 years
Multiple Disabilities				
Special class	10	6 years	N/A	N/A
Resource class	10	6 years	7	6 years

(4) If a teacher of exceptional children provides services through the collaboration model, the maximum caseload shall not exceed twenty children and youth with disabilities for grades nine–twelve, and fifteen children and youth with disabilities for grades primary–eight.
(6) If a caseload or class size exceeds the maximum specified in this administrative regulation for fifteen school days, the principal, or the school council, if the school has implemented school-based decision making, shall ask the superintendent to request an exemption or waiver from the State Board for Elementary and Secondary Education pursuant to KRS 157.360 and 156.160.

LOUISIANA

I. Bulletin 1706: Pupil/Teacher, Pupil/Speech Therapist, Teacher/Teacher Aide, and Pupil Appraisal Ratios for Public Education

A. Self-Contained Classroom

	Preschool*	Elementary	Secondary
Blindness	4–7	4–9	4–9
Deaf-blindness	2–4	2–4	2–4
Multiple disabilities	4–7	4–9	4–9
Partial seeing	6–11	8–15	8–17

Half-day categorical Preschool Class: The pupil/teacher ratio for all half-day categorical preschool classes, excluding gifted, is eight to sixteen.

B. Paraprofessional Training Units

Preschool-Aged Students: One teacher and two paraprofessionals for the initial six preschool students. For students functioning within the severe/profound range, there shall be one additional paraprofessional for any additional group of three not to exceed two additional groups of such students (maximum of four paraprofessionals per unit). For students functioning within the mild/moderate range, the additional paraprofessionals shall be added for each additional group of four. The maximum number of students may not exceed twelve.

School-Aged Students: One teacher and two paraprofessionals for the initial six students with severe/profound or low incidence disabilities, provided that after the initial six there shall be one additional paraprofessional for any additional group of three, not to exceed four additional groups of such students (maximum of six paraprofessionals per unit).

C. Resource Room (Generic or Categorical) and Itinerant Instruction Programs (per teacher)
1. Students with severe or low incidence impairments/disabilities   5–10
2. All other students with disabilities   12–27

Comment: Because of the travel requirements of the program, this range may be reduced by the school system to ten to nineteen when instruction is provided to "all other students with disabilities" and "gifted or talented pupils" in at least two different schools.

D. Combination Self-Contained and Resource Classrooms
1. Students with severe/low incidence impairments/disabilities   4–12
2. All other students with diabilities   4–12
3. Gifted   12–22

*G. Preschool Intervention Setting (Parent/Child Training)
1. Intervention in the home   5–15
2. Intervention in a school or center   10–19

I. Instruction in Regular Classes

1. Students with severe or low incidence impairments/disabilities   5–10

II. Teacher Aides

A. One teacher aide may be hired for each teacher hired under I-A above.
B. One teacher aide may be hired for each teacher hired under I-D.1 and 2 above provided there is a minimum of eight students receiving self-contained services in D.2 above in the combination class or a minimum of four students receiving self-contained services in D.1 above in the combination class.

---

*E and F are not included here because they are not relevant to this report.

III. Caseloads

The caseloads shall be determined according to the following.

Service Type	Number of Points Determining Caseload
Each hour of assessment	1
Each hour of supervision	1
Each hour of consultation	1

MAINE AND MARYLAND

These states do not have guidelines or regulations regarding class size or caseload.

MASSACHUSETTS

Chapter 766 Regulations for the Massachusetts Department of Education indicate no specific requirements for class sizes or caseloads per se. Chapter 5 at 502.2(b) speaks to the *number of children in any one instructional group*. It dictates:

No more than eight children shall be in any one instructional group with a teacher or other qualified professional;

No more than twelve children for each teacher or other qualified professional where such teacher or professional is assisted by one aide;

No more than sixteen children for each teacher or other qualified professionals where such teacher or professional is assisted by two aides.

MICHIGAN

R 340.1743   Visual Impaired Programs

(a) Class size shall be determined by the severity and multiplicity of the impairments of the visually impaired students. A special class with one teacher shall have an enrollment of not more than the equivalent of eight full-time students, and the teacher shall be responsible for the educational programming for not more than ten different students.

(b) The curriculum shall include instruction in orientation and mobility, assistance in early development of comprehensive communication skills, personal adjustment education, and prevocational and vocational experience. The public agency shall insure that low vision aids, excluding prescription eye glasses, are available and functioning properly.

R 340.1749   Teacher Consultant; Caseload; Responsibilities

(1) The teacher consultant for special education shall do one or more of the following:

(a) Provide instructional services to students who are enrolled in special education programs . . .

(b) Provide instructional services to a student whose handicap is such that the student may be educated effectively within a regular classroom if this service is provided to the student . . .

(c) Provide consultation to education personnel on behalf of handicapped persons on the consultant's caseload.

(d) Work as a member of the multidisciplinary evaluation team to assist in the evaluation of the educational needs of persons suspected of being handicapped.

(2) The teacher consultant shall carry an active caseload of not more than twenty-five handicapped students. All students served under this rule shall be counted as part of the caseload.

MINNESOTA AND MISSISSIPPI

These states do not have guidelines or regulations regarding class size or caseload.

MISSOURI

The standards reflect approvable class size and caseloads at any given time during the school year. Variations may be considered on request. Justification for approved variations may include, but not be limited to, consideration of the availability of certified personnel, the incidence of eligible students, their specified IEP requirements, and the availability of alternative resources for service . . . may require the assignment of a paraprofessional to a particular class as a condition of approval for a caseload exception.

	Itinerant Teacher	Resource Room	Center-based Classroom
Early Childhood Special Education—Full Time Equivalent Position	12–16	25	12–20
Multiple Disabilities; Deaf-Blind; Autistic			4–6
Visually Impaired: Hearing Impaired			5–8

The number of students to be assigned to a class is determined by use of a formula that combines the number of IEPs for which a teacher is responsible with the aggregate number of equivalent student contact hours accruing to the teacher during the day. The sum equals a caseload number that may not exceed sixty. The formula is as follows:

Number of IEPs + Contact hours ≤ Caseload Number

- The number of IEPs equals the number of IEPs the teacher is responsible for on a case manager basis and is traditionally the number reported as a teacher's caseload under current State Board Caseload Standards.
- Contact hours is a computed value, determined by dividing the total student minutes per week by the number of minutes per day the teacher has available for direct contact instruction.
- Caseload is a derived number for the formula and is defined as sixty. It is a limit and not a goal. Elementary classes will generally have a slightly smaller caseload number than secondary classes, due to the greater individual student management needs presented by younger students. In general, caseload numbers from thirty-five to fifty at elementary and forty to fifty-five at secondary are considered normal.

NEBRASKA

Title 92, Chapter 51 of the Nebraska Regulations states, in part:

005.02   Early Childhood Special Education Services (ECSE)

    005.02A   The caseload for both home-based and center-based programs shall range from eight to twenty children per full-time teaching staff member.

        005.02A1   In a center-based program, the maximum number of children with disabilities below age five served together at any one time by one staff member shall be as follows:

        005.02A1a   Children birth to eighteen months—four children

        005.02A1b   Children eighteen months to three years—six children

        005.02A1c   Children three to five years—ten children

        005.02A2   Home-based programs

        005.02A2a   Children birth to five years—ten to fifteen children

005.03   Level I—Special Education Support Services

    005.03A   The total number of school-age students served by Level I personnel per school year per full-time professional staff member shall fall within the following ranges:

005.03A1   Level I—Categorical Programs

      005.03A1I   Students with Visual Impairments—fifteen to twenty-five

005.04   Level II—Special Education Services

    005.04A   The total number of students served in Level II Classrooms per school year per full-time professional staff member shall fall within the following ranges:

      005.04A1   Level II—Categorical Programs

        005.04A1c   Students with Deaf-blindness—four to eight

        005.04A1h   Students with Multiple Disabilities—four to eight

        005.04A1n   Students with Visual Impairments—six to twelve

    005.04B   Level I and Level II Combination Programs

Programs that serve both Level I and Level II students may be operated. The caseload for such a combined program shall range from fifteen to twenty-five students per school year per full-time professional staff member. Students with disabilities receiving an aggregate of less than three hours of special education service per week shall be considered Level I students for purposes of reimbursement computation.

NEVADA

Nevada Administrative Code 388.150: Maximum number of cases per teacher in unit; maximum size of class; exceptions.

1. Except as otherwise provided in this section, the maximum number of cases per teacher in a unit for:
   (c) The deaf and blind is four.
   (j) Pupils with visual impairments is sixteen.
2. The maximum number of cases per teacher in a unit for itinerant home-based early childhood education or related services must be determined in the course of developing the individualized educational program for each pupil in the unit, on the basis of geographic considerations and according to the needs of each pupil and his or her parents.
3. In a departmentalized program, the maximum number of cases per teacher is to be determined according to the number of individualized educational programs for which each teacher is responsible.
4. Except as otherwise provided in this section, the maximum size of a class per instructional period for:
   (a) The hearing impaired, orthopedically impaired, severely or profoundly mentally retarded, visually impaired, seriously emotionally disturbed, or pupils with multiple impairments, autism, or a health impairment described in subsection 1 of NAC 388.402 is six.
   (c) Pupils who are deaf and blind is four.
   (h) Pupils in early childhood programs for pupils with:
      (1) Hearing impairments, visual impairments, moderate mental retardation, serious emotional disturbances, orthopedic impairments, a health impairment described in subsection 1 of NAC 388.402, and multiple impairments is six.
6. The maximum enrollment in a unit may be increased by ten percent or at least one pupil, without prior approval of the department.
7. If a teacher's aide is used in a unit, the maximum size of a class in the unit may be increased by not more than:
   (a) Four pupils in a unit for pupils who have multiple impairments or a health impairment described in subsection 1 of NAC 388.402 or are gifted; and talented, hearing impaired, learning disabled, mildly or moderately mentally retarded, orthopedically impaired, seriously emotionally disturbed, speech and language impaired, or visually impaired.
8. The maximum number of cases per teacher in each unit for a specific disability must not exceed the number of prescribed pursuant to this section for a disability represented by the majority of pupils in the unit even if some or all of the pupils in the unit attend classes in a regular educational environment and the special education teacher only provides collaborative or consulting services regarding such pupils.

9. Exceptions to the maximum enrollments prescribed in this section may be made with the written approval of the department.

NEW HAMPSHIRE

New Hampshire does not have guidelines or regulations regarding class size or caseload.

NEW JERSEY

The New Jersey Administrative Code N.J.A.C. 6:28—4.4 (a) 6 xvi limits the age span in special class programs to four years and for programs serving students who are visually impaired, the class size is limited to eight pupils. Maximum class sizes may be increased no more than one-third with the addition of a classroom aide (or a second classroom aide where one is already required).

NEW MEXICO

State Board of Education Regulations No. 92-1, Amendment 1: Student/Staff Ratios in Special Education

A. The student/staff ratio shall not exceed thirty-five for a special education teacher and sixty for a speech-language pathologist for special education programs in which properly licensed professionals travel from class to class or school to school (IEP) requires a minimal amount of special education. A minimal amount of special education services shall not exceed ten percent of the school day/week

B. The student/staff ratio shall not exceed twenty-four for a special education teacher and thirty-five for a speech-language pathologist for special education programs in which properly licensed professionals provide services to children with disabilities whose IEPs require a moderate amount of special education. A moderate amount of the special education services shall be less than fifty percent of the school day.

C. The student/staff ratio shall not exceed fifteen for special education programs in which properly licensed professionals provide services to children with disabilities whose IEPs require an extensive amount of special education for a portion of the school day as appropriate to implement a student's IEP. An extensive amount of special education services shall be provided fifty percent or more of the school day.

D. The student/staff ratio shall not exceed eight for special education programs in which a properly licensed professional provides services to children with disabilities whose IEPs require a maximum amount of special education. A maximum amount of special education services shall be provided in an amount approaching a full school day.

E. The student/adult ratio shall not exceed four for center-based special education programs in which one of the adults in the programs is a properly licensed professional providing three- and four-year old children with the amount of special education needed to implement a child's IEP. The student/adult ratio shall not exceed two for center-based special programs in which three- and four-year old children have profound educational needs.

F. Adequate student/staff ratios must be provided to appropriately address student needs identified in the IEPs. Educational assistance may provide direct services under the supervision of licensed personnel.

NEW YORK

New York does not have guidelines or regulations regarding class size or caseload. Teachers determine caseloads.

NORTH CAROLINA

.1516 Maximum Class Size: Pupil/Teacher Ratio

Local educational agencies must assure that all levels of the continuum of programs and services as defined in section .1515(E) are available, considered and utilized for all categories of children with special needs; in addition, the maximum class size in the settings below shall not be exceeded. Deviations may be made only with the prior written approval of the Division of Exceptional Children's Services upon request by a local educational agency. Local educational agencies are encouraged to lower the maximum class sizes, if needed, to meet the needs of their particular students.

Class Size: Pupil/Teacher Ratio—School-age*

Category	Level of Continuum	Maximum Class Size Number of Assistants		
		0	1	2
Deaf-Blind	Regular class (Elementary)	35 TCL		
Multi-handicapped	Regular class (Middle-secondary)	60 TCL		
	Resource class	12 no more than 35 TCL		
	Separate class		6	8
Visually Impaired	Regular class	20 TCL		
	Resource			
	Separate class	8 no more than 20 TCL		
	Residential	8		

*Total class load (TCL) for middle and high school subject area teachers (e.g., math, English) can be based on resource class size multiplied by five periods.

NORTH DAKOTA

North Dakota's *Service Guidelines for Individuals with Visual Impairments* is an adaptation of a tool used in Colorado, Utah, California, and Oregon school districts to assist in planning the services needed for visually impaired individuals. The purpose of the guidelines is twofold:

1. To determine the amount of vision related services that are required to meet the individual's needs (braille instruction, technology, environmental adaptations, orientation and mobility . . .)
2. To determine the needed resources such as personnel (vision teacher, paraprofessional, braillist . . .) and equipment and materials (technology, low vision devices, large print/braille books, curriculum adaptations. . .).

Due to the ongoing changes of an individual's curriculum, health, social/emotional status, and vocational plans, the guidelines will be used as part of the IEP process.

Rating Scale

The individual is assigned a rating of 0 to 4 in each of the following areas: medical, reading medium, compensatory skill needs, and environmental and instructional adjustments. The ratings are then added together to obtain a total score for that individual. The total score is reflective of the amount of vision-related service that the individual will need for the upcoming year. *Note:* Services may be obtained from a vision teacher (public school or NDSB), paraprofessional, braillist, orientation and mobility instructor, and/or participating in the North Dakota School for the Blind specialized programs.

Ratings/Descriptions

A. Medical
0 Normal visual acuity with full visual field, no significant pathology.
1 Possible progressive disease, but one eye still within normal limits; mild nystagmus; bilateral strabismus, which cannot be corrected: pre/post eye surgery; other severe temporary eye treatments, such as patching; significant bilateral field loss.
2 Acuity 20/70 to 20/200 in best eye after correction, a visual field of more than twenty degrees.
3 Acuity 20/200 to object perception in best eye after correction, a visual field of twenty degrees or less.
4 Object perception to total blindness, a visual field of ten degrees or less; cortical blindness.

B. Reading Medium (or Estimated Future Reading Medium)

0   Regular print with no modification; multihandicapped nonreader
1   Regular print with magnification in addition to correction
2   Regular print with consistent use of magnification in addition to correction
3   Tape or large print
4   Tape or braille

C. Compensatory Skill Needs/Adaptive or Developmental Training

0   Needs no compensatory skills instruction; needs academic tutoring.
1   Needs compensatory skill instruction in handwriting, fine and gross motor areas, PE/recreational activities, basic concept development, functional daily living skills, and/or orientation and mobility.
2   Needs compensatory skill instruction in use of residual vision, sensory awareness, calculator usage, pre-vocational skills, use of adaptive equipment, and/or orientation and specific location.
3   Needs compensatory skill instruction in concept development, use of low vision devices, computer/typing, map reading, geographical and science concepts; and/or career and vocational training.
4   Needs compensatory skill instruction in tactual development, braille, use of low vision devices, abacus, slate and stylus, daily living skills, and/or orientation and mobility.

D. Environmental Instructional Adjustments

0   Needs no adaptations of instructional materials or presentations.
1   Needs some adapted written materials, dark copies, special seating, some magnification, adaptive lighting, materials storage area, work area for special equipment, adapting material and communication system, technology, leisure/recreation, and/or positioning.
2   Needs occasional use of tapes, some adaptation of maps/graphs, frequent magnification, and/or adaptive lighting.
3   Needs tapes, enlargement, or adaptation of maps/graph, pictures, etc., close seating, consistent magnification, and/or adaptive lighting.
4   Needs braille, tactual materials, complete adaptation of instructional materials, cannot visually benefit from classroom films, demonstrations, needs extra time allowance for assignments, and/or needs a modified curriculum.

Interpretations

0–1 Total Points (No Service)—means that this individual may be monitored by their optometrist or ophthalmologist. No services from a vision teacher are necessary.

2–6 Total Points (Consultation Service)—This is an individual with mild needs who will benefit from a low degree of consultation services provided by a vision teacher to an individual, education personnel, and parents.

7–9 Total Points (Light Itinerant Service)—This is an individual who has moderate needs. This individual needs a higher amount of consultation services and may benefit from direction instruction.

10–12 Total Points (Heavy Itinerant Service)—This is an individual who needs direct instruction and a moderate amount of curricular adaptations. Classroom consultation continues to be intense.

13–16 Total Points (Resource)—This is an individual who will need intense direct instruction and extensive adaptations in multiple specialized areas (braille, daily living skills, orientation and mobility, technology, careers).

When determining an appropriate caseload, a number of variables have been determined within the guidelines. These variables include direct instruction, consultation time to staff and parents, securing and adapting materials, attending meetings, and writing reports. Travel time needs to be considered when determining appropriate caseload. It is recommended that a full-time caseload does not exceed fifty-six points. In addition, no vision teacher should have more than two braille users on a caseload. It is important to remember that this is a guideline and that there is always flexibility in determining what is an appropriate caseload.

OHIO

The Ohio Department of Education's Rules for the Education of Handicapped Children states:

3301-51-03

A. 2. Teacher/Pupil Ratio

a. The supplemental services teacher shall serve a minimum of fifteen eligible children placed full-time in regular classes. Additional handicapped children above the required minimum caseload, but within the fifteen to thirty case load range, who are integrated into regular classrooms from special class/learning centers on a part-time basis may also be served by the supplemental services teacher.

C. 2. Teacher/Pupil Ratio

a. Individual instruction. The individual instruction teacher shall not serve more than one child during any single instructional period.

D. 2. Teacher/Pupil Ratio

The minimum and maximum number of children for a special class/learning center shall be as specified for each category within rule 3301-51-01 of the Administrative Code.

3301-51-04

A. Program for Multihandicapped Children

3.c.(i)(a) One special class/learning center teacher shall serve six to eight children.

C. Program for Visually Handicapped Children

3.c.(i) Teacher/pupil ratio

(a) One special class/learning center teacher shall serve six to ten children.

(b) No more than eight children shall be served during any one instructional period.

OKLAHOMA

The policies and procedures booklet from the Oklahoma Department of Education states: "Class size for all placements in special education shall be no more than ten at any time." There is nothing in the actual regulations regarding class size.

OREGON

The class sizes and caseloads are based on state and national averages for agencies to use as a general guide in establishing local caseloads and class sizes. These ranges should not be viewed as established minimum state requirements. For State Level Funding it is 1:9, but this is not in their regulations. The caseload guidelines vary by exceptionality area. For the area of visual impairment, the following ranges are used.

Type of Program	Class Size and Caseload Ranges
Resource room (one teacher and one aide)	8 to 12 students
Self-contained classrooms (one teacher and one aide):	
Infants or preschool	4 to 8 students
Kindergarten through third grade	6 to 10 students
Fourth through twelfth grade	8 to 12 students
Multihandicapped	3 to 7 students
Itinerant teacher	8 to 12 students
Orientation and mobility instructor	8 to 12 students
Home-based infants or preschool age	13 to 17 students

RHODE ISLAND

Within the state of Rhode Island, services for blind and visually impaired students are delivered primarily through:

1. Teachers employed by the larger communities (currently five teachers).
2. Teachers employed by the Department of Education who travel throughout the remaining communities (currently four teachers).

There is no specific language within the state regulations regarding class size or caseloads; however, there is some language contained within the contracts for teachers employed by the Department of Education.

SOUTH CAROLINA

For the South Carolina School for the Blind:

Programs	Student : Teacher Ratio
Self-Contained	
Preschool	3 : 1
Elementary	8 : 1
Middle School	10 : 1
High School	
There are teacher assistants and teacher aides available for assisting teachers at every grade level who rotate their services depending on individual students' needs	
Itinerant with Mainstream Classes	
Elementary	8 : 1
Junior High and High School	15 : 1
Orientation and Mobility Instructors	Upcoming to 20 students (depending on travel time and number of sessions per week)
Braille Teacher	22 braille readers
Low Vision Specialist (consultation only)	50–55 students

For public school programs:

	Maximum Ratio (Based on Average Daily Membership)	
Self-Contained Classes		
(may be mainstreamed one period per day)	10 : 1	K-6
	12 : 1	7/8
	12 : 1	9-12
Itinerant and Resource Room	**Maximum Caseload**	
	15	All Grades

SOUTH DAKOTA

There are no regulations; however, the South Dakota School for the Visually Handicapped does have guidelines for its Outreach Department.

CASELOADS (establishment of)

1. The territory covered by each consultant will be established cooperatively by the administration and consultants. With three consultants the territory will be split so that one person covers the northeastern part of the state, one the southeastern, and one the west. Location of the consultants' base will be determined by the administration.
2. Caseloads will be established for each consultant subject to final approval by the principal. A maximum caseload has been established to ensure adequate service. The "Active 1" caseload for any consultant during one quarter will be thirty students.

A. Additions to the caseloads may be made by referral through outreach consultants and liaison for services with concurrence of the principal.

B Prior to any assignment, current caseloads and proximity to other students receiving service will be evaluated. This will be determined cooperatively by the administration and the outreach consultant.

C No child will be added to an outreach consultant's regular caseload unless the child has had a current ophthalmological evaluation.

D When any consultant's caseload is at capacity, a waiting list will be established, factored on both date of application and severity of need. Preference will be given to students who do not have access to vision services within their own school districts. School districts and parents will be kept informed.

3. The outreach consultant will code his or her caseload as follows:

A *Referral:*
Receipt of name and start date collection.

B *Active—1:*
Regular visits (two weeks to once per year) and professional consultations/single visits.

C *Active—2:*
No services for one to two years; file remains with consultant.

4. Each outreach consultant will provide caseload information to the principal and superintendent on the report form four times a year: September 15, December 15, March 15, and May 15.

TENNESSEE

The Options of Services are recommendations only—and not to statute or required of the LEAs. Furthermore, these options are not specific to blindness and visual impairments, but are universally applicable to all areas of special education.

Option	Description	Contact Hours	Caseload/Class Size
Option 1	a. Consulting Teacher b. Direct Services c. Related Services	a. Consults with regular teacher at least twice a month b. Less than 1 hour per week c. At least twice a month and less than one hour per week (3 times a year OT/PT)	a. 75 students b. 75 students c. 75 students
Option 2	Direct Instructional Services	1–3 hours per week	60 students for 1 teacher 30 additional students for 1 aide
Option 3	Resource Program	4–8 hours per week	38 students for 1 teacher 19 additional students for 1 aide
Option 4	Resource Program	9–13 hours per week	21 students for 1 teacher 11 additional students for 1 aide
Option 5	Resource Program	14–22 hours per week	12 students for 1 teacher 6 additional students for 1 aide
Option 6	Ancillary Person	4 hours per day in the regular classroom	2 students
Option 7	Developmental Class/ Mainstreamed	23 or more hours per week	8 students for 1 teacher 4 additional students for 1 aide
Option 8	Self-Contained Comprehensive Development Class	32.5 or more hours per week *including* 2 related services	5 students for 1 teacher 2 additional students for 1 aide
Option 9	Residential Program	24 hours per day	
Option 10	Homebound/Hospital Instruction	3 hours per week	8 students

* Option 8: The 32.5 hours can include up to 10 hours per week of Special Education Aide in the regular program.

TEXAS

Texas does not have any regulations or guidelines that address class size or caseloads for students with disabilities. However, many districts choose to use a caseload analysis process that is part of *Quality Programs for Students with Visual Impairments* which was developed by Nancy Toelle. This Program is available through the Outreach Department at the Texas School for the Blind.

UTAH

State of Utah Special Education Rules state that the size of self-contained vision classes shall not exceed twelve and the headcount for active teachers' caseload (itinerant teachers for the visually impaired) shall not exceed twenty.

The Utah School for the Deaf and Blind Administration tries to keep the size of self-contained classes between six to twelve with an aide. The outreach teachers and itinerant personnel have a caseload of twenty and when caseloads become too large, measures are taken to increase positions or full-time equivalencies (FTEs).

VERMONT

Caseloads are determined by the population area and the topography. Of the six itinerant teachers in Vermont, the lowest caseload is twenty-seven and the highest is fifty, though these caseloads are flexible and vary as students are identified and/or traveling becomes a major part of the teacher's day.

VIRGINIA

Virginia does not have legislation determining caseloads for students with a visual disability, though it does for other disabilities. To provide guidance to their teachers of the visually impaired, Virginia relies on the American Foundation for the Blind's *Program Planning and Evaluation for Blind and Visually Impaired Students: National Guidelines for Educational Excellence* (Hazekamp and Huebner).

WASHINGTON

In Washington services provided are decided at the local district level in accordance with state and federal guidelines for all disability categories. Services across the state are typically itinerant with caseloads varying from fifteen to forty.

WEST VIRGINIA

The School for the Blind and the public schools follow these same regulations.

2. The maximum caseloads for teachers providing special education services for students with autism, blind and partial sight, deafness-blindness, deafness and other hearing impairments, giftedness, other health impairments, preschool special needs, speech/language impairments, and traumatic brain injuries placed in regular education, full-time or regular education, part-time are as follows:

   c. Blind and Partially Sighted

      1) Regular Education: Full-time—Assign no more than thirty students

      2) Regular Education: Part-time—Assign no more than fifteen students with a limit of five during any one instructional period.

      3) Special Education: Separate Class

         (a) Assign no more than five students without a full-time aide with a limit of five during any one instructional period.

         (b) Assign no more than ten students with a full-time aide with a limit of ten (10) during any one instructional period.

   d. Deaf-Blind

1) Regular Education: Full-time—Assign no more than twenty students.
2) Regular Education: Part-time—Assign no more than ten students with a limit of five during any one instructional period.

WISCONSIN

Maximum enrollments are to be viewed by the local educational agencies as the largest number of students to be served by that program type and level without special DHCPS approval. *Note:* The enrollment maximums must include all students with exceptional educational needs (EEN) appropriately placed in the unit on the basis of the IEP, including those students whose identified disabilities are other than the designated categorical program or the disability area in which the special education teacher is licensed. These maximums are not meant to be synonymous with what is an appropriate enrollment or class size for all situations.

Vision

	Early Education	Primary	Intermediate	Elementary Wide Range	Middle/Junior	Senior	Secondary Wide Range
Self-contained complete (Min. 5)	All VI Students	7	7	7	9	9	11
Self-contained modified (Min. 5)	are in Generic	9	9	8	10	11	11
Self-contained integrated (Min. 7)	Early Childhood	10	10	9	11	12	12
Resource (Min. 8)	with support	—	—	12	—	—	12
Itinerant (Min. 8)	from VI Staff	—	—	15	—	—	15

WYOMING

Wyoming has no regulations pertaining to class size or caseloads nor do they have any guidelines regarding these items.

NATIONAL SURVEY

Submitted by Association of Instructional
Resource Centers for the Visually Handicapped (AIRCVH)
Prepared by Suzanne A. Dalton

This national survey was conducted to address implementation of Goal 7: Access to developmental and educational services will include an assurance that instructional materials are available to students in the appropriate media and at the same time as their sighted peers.

Of the 150 surveys distributed, a total of thirty survey responses were received. Those responses represented information from the following twenty-seven states: **Alaska, Arizona, Arkansas, California (partial), Colorado (partial), Florida, Georgia, Idaho, Indiana, Iowa, Kansas, Maryland, Massachusetts, Minnesota, Missouri, New Mexico, North Carolina, Ohio, Oregon, Pennsylvania (partial), South Carolina, South Dakota, Vermont, Virginia, Washington, Wyoming, and West Virginia.** The analysis of the data will be conducted on information received from 54 percent of the states.

SURVEY QUESTIONS: PROVISION OF MATERIALS

1. How many visually impaired students is your center/agency currently serving?

Number of federal quota students	17,294
Number of other students (including partially sighted students)	7,379
TOTAL number of students served	24,673

2. To whom does your center/agency provide specialized materials (texts) and/or equipment? Check all that are appropriate.

Students enrolled in residential schools	19
Students enrolled in public school programs	25
Students enrolled in private school programs	20
Students enrolled in agency early childhood or adult educational programs	25
Please list other applicable programs:	2
• parents who are blind	
• teachers who are blind	1
• home-schooled students	2

3. Does your state have a statute and/or official policy that grants automatic copyright permission for transcription of specialized materials? Check all that apply.

Braille transcription	11
Large-print production	10
Audio production	7
Electronic texts	4

4. How much does your center/agency expend annually for specialized materials and equipment (fiscal year costs)? Total is *not* to include staff salaries, personnel benefits, office supplies, indirect costs, etc.

Federal quota	$1,541,000.00 (42%)
Federal, IDEA Part B	$ 587,000.00 (16%)
State funds	$1,554,900.00 (42%)
Please list other governmental revenue source(s)	None
TOTAL dollars expended on specialized materials	$3,682,900.00 (100%)

5. Does your center/agency generate revenues from alternative funding sources and/or non-traditional partnerships?

Corporate/business support	None
Foundation support/trust funds	$528,400.00 (5 states)
Sales to other center/agencies/schools	$210,000.00 (4 states)
Please list other non-traditional revenue source(s)	
• Volunteer group	$ 5,000.00 (1 state)

6. Does your center/agency utilize volunteers to produce specialized materials (include braille, large print, audio and electronic format)? Check all that apply.

Trained volunteers (individuals or groups)	14
Prison industries program	7
Prison educational or vocational program	7
Please list other volunteer programs:	
• Boy Scouts/Girl Scouts	2
• Radio Reading	1

7. What is the estimated worth of the specialized materials produced by your state's volunteers, annually (based on a contract rate of $2.50 per braille page)? $11,987,568.00 (11 states)

8. What is the average time span (in number of weeks) between the time of initial materials order and completed materials delivery? (Please include working papers used to calculate these estimates.)

In May of each year	4½ to 5 weeks
In July of each year	6½ to 7 weeks
In September of each year	5½ to 6 weeks

9. How does your center/agency track the length of time between initial order and materials delivery? Please complete applicable responses.

Commercial software used—8
(2 = Excel; 2 = Access; 2 = unspecified; 1 = Filemaker Pro; 1 = PFS Professional file)

Customized software—8
(4 = Unspecified; 2 = ESIMACS; 1 = Library software; 1 = Alpha 4)

Hardware uses	16
(2 = Mainframes; 14 = PCs)	
Manual method	14

10. Does your center/agency follow up with materials' users on a regular basis asking if materials are still needed? (Circle Y or N.) If "yes," how often?   Y = 14 N = 7

(6 = annually; 2 = three to six months; 1 = monthly; 1 = weekly; 1 = routinely)

11. Does your center/agency loan materials to other state centers and/or other school districts across the country? (Circle Y or N)   Y = 11 N = 12

If "yes," how many materials does your center loan annually?
40 to 50 titles = 2; 30 titles = 1; 20 titles = 2; 5 to 10 titles = 2; 3 to 5 titles = 4

For questions 12 to 16, *the total percentage calculated for each question should equal 100%.* The term "materials orders" is defined as textbooks, workbooks, enrichment worksheets, teacher-made materials, test/assessment instruments, etc.

12. What percentage of materials orders for *braille* are filled by:

	0–20%	21–40%	41–60%	61–80%	81–100%
Federal quota/APH	17	4	0	1	2
Outside purchase via vendors	6	10	5	2	0
In-stock items	5	11	3	0	0
Internal production (incl. volunteers)	11	5	1	1	0
Borrowed items	13	1	0	0	0
Orders not filled (incl. canceled orders)	10	1	0	0	0
Please list others, as applicable: External Production	1	0	0	0	0

13. What percentage of materials orders for *large print* are filled by:

	0–20%	21–40%	41–60%	61–80%	81–100%
Federal quota/APH	13	4	2	1	3
Outside purchase via vendors	11	1	3	1	0
In-stock items	4	8	7	0	0
Internal production (incl. volunteers)	7	6	2	2	0
Borrowed items	8	1	0	0	0
Orders not filled (incl. canceled orders)	8	1	0	0	0
Please list others, as applicable: In-state Production Facility	0	1	0	0	0

14. What percentage of materials orders for *recorded versions* are filled by:

	0–20%	21–40%	41–60%	61–80%	81–100%
Federal quota/APH	3	0	0	0	1
Outside purchase via vendors	6	0	0	1	0
In-stock items	4	2	1	0	0
Internal production (incl. volunteers)	8	1	0	0	0
Borrowed items/RFB & D	0	2	3	1	9
Orders not filled (incl. canceled orders)	2	0	0	0	0
Please list others, as applicable:	None				

15. What percentage of materials orders for *electronic format* are filled by:

	0–20%	21–40%	41–60%	61–80%	81–100%
Federal quota/APH	0	0	1	0	2
Outside purchase via vendors	2	0	1	0	1
In-stock items	1	0	0	0	0
Internal production (incl. volunteers)	0	0	0	1	0
Borrowed items	0	0	0	0	0
Orders not filled (incl. canceled orders)	0	0	0	0	0
Please list others, as applicable:	None				

16. What percentage of orders for *educational aids and/or specialized equipment including materials for those with multiple disabilities* are filled by:

	0–20%	21–40%	41–60%	61–80%	81–100%
Federal quota/APH	2	8	4	4	5
Outside purchase via vendors	12	3	2	1	0
In-stock items	3	4	3	3	1
Internal production (incl. volunteers)	2	1	0	0	0
Borrowed items	4	0	0	0	0

	0–20%	21–40%	41–60%	61–80%	81–100%
Orders not filled (incl. canceled orders)	6	0	0	0	0
Please list others, as applicable:					
Teacher-produced	1	0	0	0	0

17. What procedures are in place to ensure that access to print using optical devices (as appropriate) are included in all considerations of appropriate media for students? Are low vision evaluations included in these procedures? Who pays for prescribed devices? Are students with multiple disabilities eligible to receive these services? Please include a description of the referral process.

> **SERVICES:** Access to optical devices = 12; access to low vision evaluations = 12; learning media assessment required = 3; multi-impaired included = 5
>
> **WHO PAYS?** LEAs = 12; parents = 9; state rehabilitation agency = 7; insurance = 2; service organizations = 2; grant = 1
>
> **REFERRAL PROCESS:** LEA to school for the blind = 5; LEA to rehabilitation agency = 2; provision of regularly scheduled low vision clinics = 2

18. On the September 15, 1996, estimate what percentage of visually impaired students will have the *same materials as their sighted peers* in their preferred specialized format (braille, large print, audio, etc.)? What factors influence this materials delivery?

0–20%	21–40%	41–60%	61–80%	81–100%
0	3	2	4	14

> **FACTORS:** Late orders = 9; lack of sources = 5; lack of funds = 4; LEA text adoption timelines = 4; subject matter = 3; copyright problems = 3; student schedules = 2; new students = 2; length of braille production process = 2; high number of orders = 1; block scheduling = 1

19. What procedures are in place to ensure that visually impaired students receive materials *at the same time* as their sighted peers?

> **PROCEDURES:** Early orders encouraged = 14; reminder letters sent = 7; FAPE, IEP, or Braille Bill standards = 4; vendor contact = 1; performance evaluation of staff = 1; multiple transcription methods = 2

20. **Please send copies of any state law and/or state education policies relating to specialized materials for students with visual impairments.** Examples may include: (a) Authorizing legislation for provision of specialized materials; (b) State textbook adoption policies (if one of twenty-two adoption states); (c) Braille Bill; (d) Copyright permission statute; and (e) Any applicable initiatives/rules/bills currently pending at the state level.

> **Received information from:** Arizona, Arkansas, California, Florida, Georgia, Indiana, Kansas, New Mexico, Ohio, Oregon, Virginia

21. Are specialized materials (e.g., braille, large print, recorded, and/or electronic texts) produced by "volunteers" in your state? If "no," please skip to question 29.
    Yes = 18   No = 6

22. Is Library of Congress certification required of all volunteers producing braille?
    Yes = 12   No = 5
    If "no," what percentage of braillists are NOT certified? 0–10% = 2; 60% = 1

23. Which of the listed guidelines/standards are followed in the volunteer production of the specialized materials in your state? Check all that are applicable.

    16 Library of Congress
    14 Literacy Code
    15 Textbook Code
    14 Nemeth Code
    9 Music Code

   9   Computer Notation Code
  11   National Braille Association
  10   Braille Authority of North America
   3   American Printing House for the Blind
   3   Recording for the Blind
   4   California Transcribers and Educators of the Visually Handicapped
   1   Other (list): guidelines of individual volunteer group

24. Are any "quick and dirty" specialized materials produced by volunteers (that is, materials that do not specifically follow guidelines/standards listed in question 21?)   Yes = 11   No = 10

    If "yes," what is the estimated percentage of "quick and dirty" materials produced?
    1% = 2; 5% = 2; 10% = 2; 20% = 1; 30% = 1

    If "yes," are these materials produced this way for the benefit of the student at the request of a certified teacher of the visually impaired?   Yes = 10   No = 2

25. Are tactile graphics routinely included in texts?   Yes = 17   No = 3

    If "yes," what guidelines are followed in the production of tactile graphics?

    GUIDELINES: Library of Congress = 4; NBA = 2; teacher guidelines = 2; AFB Tactile Graphics = 2; BANA = 1; CTEVH = 1; APH Graphics Kit = 1; transcriber group guidelines = 1; IRC guidelines = 1

26. How is accuracy of transcription assured in each of the media listed below?

    Braille: Paid proofreaders = 9; braillists proofread = 6; teacher/reader feedback = 5; spot checks = 1; braille editors review = 1; proofreading software = 1

    Large Print: Quality checks = 6; teacher/reader feedback = 4

    Recorded: Spot checks = 3; proofreading = 2; teacher/reader feedback = 2; RFB & D monitors = 1

    Electronic texts: Proofreading = 1; teacher/reader feedback = 1

27. Are volunteer-produced specialized materials routinely proofread prior to sending materials to user? If "no," please skip to question 28.

    Yes = 15   No = 6

28. How are the volunteer-produced specialized materials proofread (e.g., spell-check software, Library of Congress certified proofreader, etc.)?

    Certified proofreader = 11; software = 7; braillists proofread = 5; teachers proofread = 1

29. Who pays for proofreading, if applicable?   IRC or SEA = 8; volunteer group = 4

30. How is data collected concerning the quality of materials from users of volunteer-produced materials?

    Formal/informal survey of teachers/administrators = 10; user feedback = 6

31. In the purchasing of specialized materials from various vendors, prioritize the criteria listed below that are used in the selection of supplier?

    The number of priority #1s:

    5   price of materials
    3   speed of delivery/turnaround time
    5   appropriate format
    0   guidelines/standards followed
    3   overall quality of braille output
    0   tactile graphics in braille
    0   standard point size for large print
    0   tone indexing for recorded materials

0   description of figures for recorded materials
0   labeling of materials
2   Other (list): availability
1   Other (list): good reputation of vendor
1   Other (list): availability on quota

32. How is data collected concerning the quality of purchased materials?

Formal/informal survey of teachers/administrators = 15; user feedback = 8; conversations with vendors = 2

ADVISORY BOARD

Kate Aldrich, Parent
National Association for Parents of the Visually Impaired, Santa Rosa, CA

Dr. Anne L. Corn, Professor of Special Education, Ophthalmology and Visual Sciences
Vanderbilt University, Nashville, TN

Dr. Joy Efron, Coordinating Principal
Program for Visually Impaired Students, Los Angeles Unified School District, Los Angeles, CA

Warren Figueiredo, Resource Specialist
Braille and Technology Center, Louisiana School for the Visually Impaired, Baton Rouge, LA

Dr. Phil Hatlen, Superintendent
Texas School for the Blind and Visually Impaired, Austin, TX

Dr. Kathleen Mary Huebner, Assistant Dean
Graduate Program in Education and Rehabilitation, Institute for the Visually Impaired, Pennsylvania College of Optometry, Philadelphia, PA

Mary Nell McLennan, Director
Education and Advisory Services, American Printing House for the Blind, Louisville, KY

Sue Melrose, Computer Access Consultant
New Berlin, WI

Herb Miller, Superintendent
St. Joseph's School for the Blind, Jersey City, NJ

Kevin E. O'Connor, Past President
National Association for Parents of the Visually Impaired, Hawthorne Woods, IL

Frank Ryan, National Program Associate in Education
American Foundation for the Blind, San Francisco, CA

Mary Ann Siller, National Program Associate in Education
American Foundation for the Blind, Dallas, TX

Jay Stiteley, Field Services Representative
The Seeing Eye, Inc., Morristown, NJ

Donna Stryker
National Association for Parents of the Visually Impaired, Las Cruces, NM

Dr. Karen Wolffe
Career Counseling and Consultation, Manchaca, TX

STATE COORDINATORS

Alabama
Jim Stoval, Director
Grants and Projects
Institutional Advancement
P.O. Box 698
Talladega, AL 35161
(205) 761-3262 Fax (205) 761-3337

Alaska
William McIver, Educ. Specialist
Special Education Service Agency
2217 E. Tudor Road, Suite 1
Anchorage, AK 99507
(907) 562-7372 Fax (907) 562-0545

Arizona
Jane Erin, Professor
University of Arizona
Dept. of Special Education
Education Building 69
Tuscon, AZ 85721
(520) 621-0945 Fax (520) 621-3821

Arkansas
Bob Brasher, State Coordinator
Educ. Services for Visually Impaired
Arkansas School for the Blind
P.O. Box 668
Little Rock, AR 72203
(501) 296-1815 Fax (501) 663-3536

California
Sharon Sacks, Education Director
Pupil Personnel Services
California School for the Blind
500 Walnut Avenue

Fremont, CA 94536
(510) 794-3800 Fax (510) 794-3813

Steve Goodman, Director
Pupil Personnel Services
California School for the Blind
500 Walnut Avenue
Freemont, CA 94536
(510) 794-3800 Fax (510) 794-3813

Colorado
David Farrell, Coordinator
Educ. Services for the Blind
33 North Institute Street
Colorado Springs, CO 80903
(719) 578-2100 Fax (719) 578-2239

Lucia Hasty, Consultant
Instructional Materials Center
  for the Visually Handicapped
1015 High Street
Colorado Springs, CO 80903
(719) 578-2195 Fax (719) 578-2239

Delaware
Lynne Young, Education Supervisor
Divisions for the Visually Impaired
305 West 8th Street
Wilmington, DE 19801
(302) 577-3333

Florida
Carol Allman, Program Specialist
Florida Education Center, Room 601
325 West Gaines Street
Tallahassee, FL 32399-0400
(904) 488-3103 Fax (904) 922-7088

Georgia
Marie Amerson, Teacher Consultant
LEA/Georgia Academy for the Blind
2895 Vineville Avenue
Macon, GA 31204-2899
(912) 744-6083

Idaho
Ron Darcy, Superintendent
Idaho School for the Deaf and the Blind
1450 Main Street
Gooding, ID 83330
(208) 934-4457 Fax (208) 934-8352

Illinois
Alice Post, Manager
Illinois Instruction Materials Center
3031 Stanton
Springfield, IL 62703-4316
(217) 525-3300

Indiana
Judith Whyte, Director of Outreach
Indiana School for the Blind
7725 North College Avenue
(317) 253-1481 Fax (317) 251-6511

Sharon Knoth
Indiana Dept. of Education
Division of Special Education
Room 229, State House
Indianapolis, IN 46204-2798
(317) 232-0581 Fax (317) 232-0589

Iowa
Dotta Hassman, Coordinator
Instructional Materials Center
Iowa Braille and Sight Saving School
1002 G Avenue
Vinton, IA 52349
(319) 472-5221 Fax (319) 472-4371

Kansas
Jacqueline Denk, Coordinator
Instructional Resource Center
1100 State Avenue
Kansas City, KS 66102
(913) 281-3308 Fax (913) 281-3104

Kentucky
Linda Smith, State Coordinator
Educational Services for Visually Impaired
    Students
Kentucky School for the Blind
1867 Frankfort Avenue
Louisville, KY 40206

Louisiana
Joyce Russo, Supervisor of Program for Individuals
    with Deaf-Blindness
Louisiana Department of Education
P.O. Box 94064
Baton Rouge, LA 70804-9064
(504) 763-3590 (504) 763-3553

Maine
Jean T. Small, Program Director
Education Services for Blind and
    Visually Impaired Children
1066 Kenduskeag Avenue
Bangor, ME 04401
(207) 941-2855 Fax (207) 941-2855

Maryland
M. Loretta McGraw, LRE/Low Incidence Specialist
Department of Special Education, Room 200
200 West Baltimore Street
Baltimore, MD 21201-2595
(410) 767-0233 Fax (410) 333-8165

Massachusetts
Karen Ross, Director
Vision Associates
Carroll Center for the Blind
770 Centre Street
Newton, MA 02158
(617) 969-6200 Fax (617) 969-6204

Michigan
Kathy Brown, Principal
Michigan School for the Blind
West Court and Miller
Flint, MI 48503
(810) 257-1420 Fax (810) 257-0500

Minnesota
Jean Martin, Director
Minnesota Resource Center: Blind/VI
615 Olof Hanson Drive
Faribault, MN 55021-0308
(507) 332-3232 Fax (507) 332-5494

Elaine Sveen, Superintendent
Minnesota State Academy for the Blind
P.O. Box 68
Faribault, MN 55021-0308
(507) 332-3226 Fax (507) 332-3631

Mississippi
Rosie Thompson, Assistant Principal
Mississippi School for the Blind
1252 Eastover Drive
Jackson, MS 39211
(601) 984-8211

Missouri
Jennie Mascheck, Vision Supervisor
Outreach Services Division
Missouri School for the Blind
3815 Magnolia Avenue
St. Louis, MO 63110
(314) 776-4320 Ext. 253
Fax (314) 776-1875

Nebraska
William Mann, Superintendent
Nebraska School for the Visually Impaired
P.O. Box 129
Nebraska City, NE 68410-0129
(402) 873-5513 Fax (402) 873-3463

New Hampshire
Bill Finn, Coordinator
New Hampshire Educational Services for Sensory
    Impaired
117 Pleasant Street, Dolloff Building
Concord, NH 03301
(603) 226-2900 Fax (603) 226-2907

New Jersey
Herbert Miller, Administrator
St. Joseph's School for the Blind
253 Baldwin Avenue
Jersey City, NJ 07306
(201) 653-0578 Fax (201) 653-4087

New Mexico
Eileen Kuhre, Supervisor Outreach Services
New Mexico School for the Visually Handicapped
1900 North White Sands Boulevard
Alamogordo, NM 88310
(505) 437-3505

New York
Emily Leyenberger, Coordinator, Vision Specialist
New York State Resource Center for Visually
    Impaired
Richmond Avenue
Batavia, NY 14020
(919) 733-6381 Fax (919) 733-9289

North Carolina
George Lee, Director of Student Services
Governor Morehead School
301 Ashe Avenue
Raleigh, NC 27606
(919) 733-6381 Fax (919) 733-9289

North Dakota
Carmen Suminski, Superintendent
North Dakota School for the Blind
500 Standford Road
Grand Forks, ND 58203
(701) 795-2700 (701) 795-2727

Ohio
Marjorie Ward, Professor
School of Teaching and Learning
Ohio State University
333 Arps Hall
1945 North High Street
Columbus, OH 43210
(614) 292-2437 Fax (614) 292-7695

Paula Mauro
Resource Center for Low Incidence
470 Glenmont Avenue
Columbus, OH 43214
(614) 262-6131 Fax (614) 262-1070
paula_mauro!coserrc.esu.k12.oh.us

John Saylor, Ed.D., Coordinator
Division of Special Education
Ohio Department of Education
933 High Street
Washington, OH 43085-4087
(614) 466-2650 Fax (614) 728-1097

Oklahoma
Robert Warren, Principal
Parkview School
3300 Gibson Street
Muskogee, OK 74403
(918) 682-6641

Oregon
Ann Hicks, Superintendent
Oregon School for the Blind
700 Church Street, S.E.
Salem, OR 97301
(503) 378-3820 Fax (503) 373-7537

Pennsylvania
Diane P. Wormsley, Ph.D.
Coordinator, EVI Program
Pennsylvania College of Optometry
1200 West Godfrey Avenue
Philadelphia, PA 19141
(215) 276-6169 Fax (215) 276-6292
dwormsley@pco.edu

Cynthia Jackson Glenn
The Pennsylvania College of Optometry
1200 West Godfrey Avenue
Philadelphia, PA 19141
(215) 276-6290

Rhode Island
Clare Chartier, Coordinator
Vision Services Program
Rhode Island Department of Education
One Corliss Park
Providence, RI 02908
(401) 277-3827

South Carolina
Linda Mackechnie, Director
School for the Blind
South Carolina School for the Deaf and the Blind
355 Cedar Springs Road
Spartanburg, SC 29302
(803) 585-7711

Suzanne Swaffield, Educ. Associate
Programs for Exceptional Children
South Carolina Department of Education
1429 Senate Street, Room 513
Columbia, SC 29201
(803) 734-8222 Fax (803) 734-8624

South Dakota
Majorie Kaiser, Superintendent
South Dakota School for the Visually Handicapped
423 17th Avenue, S.E.
Aberdeen, SD 57401-7699
(605) 622-2580 Fax (605) 622-2607

Texas
Phil Hatlen, Superintendent
Texas School for Blind and Visually Impaired
1100 West 45th Street
Austin, TX 78757
(512) 454-6305

Cyral Miller, Director of Outreach
Texas School for Blind and Visually Impaired
1100 West 45th Street
Austin, TX 78757
(512) 454-6305

Utah
Lee Robinson, Superintendent
Utah Schools for the Deaf and the Blind
742 Harrison Boulevard
Ogden, UT 84404
(801) 399-9631

Vermont
Stephanie Bissonette, Lead Educator
Vermont Association for the Blind
37 Elmwood Avenue
Burlington, VT 05401
(802) 863-1358 Fax (802) 863-1481

Virginia
Barbara McCarthy, Director
Virginia Library and Resource Center for the Blind
395 Azalea Avenue
Richmond, VA 23227-3623
(804) 371-3661 Fax (804) 371-3508

Washington
Joan Christensen, Outreach Consultant
Washington Instructional Resource Center
Washington State School for the Blind
2120 East 13th Street
Vancouver, WA 98661
(360) 696-6321 Ext. 185

West Virginia
Donna See, Director
Instructional Resource Center for Visually Impaired
301 East Main Street
Romney, WV 26757
(304) 822-4800 Fax (304) 822-3370

Wisconsin
Andrew Papineau, State Consultant for Visually
    Impaired
Wisconsin Department of Public Instruction
P.O. Box 7841
Madison, WI 53707-7841
(608) 266-3522 Fax (608) 267-1052

Wyoming
Janet Wood, Director
Services for the Visually Impaired
Wyoming Department of Education
Hathaway Building, 2nd Floor
Cheyenne, WY 82002-0050
(307) 777-6257 Fax (307) 777-6234

NATIONAL GOAL LEADERS

GOAL 1: Referral
National Goal Leader: Foundation for Blind Children
1235 East Harmont Drive
Phoenix, AZ 85020
602-331-1470
Contact: Chris Tompkins

GOAL 2: Parent Participation
National Goal Leader: National Association for Parents of the Visually Impaired (NAPVI)
P.O. Box 317
Watertown, MA 02272-0317
617-972-7441
Contact: Susan LaVenture

GOAL 3: Personnel Preparation
National Goal Leader: Division 17, Association for Education and Rehabilitation of the Blind and
    Visually Impaired (AER)
c/o University of Northern Colorado, Division of Special Education
Greeley, CO 80639
303-351-2691
Contact: Dr. Kay Alicyn Ferrell

GOAL 4: Provision of Education Services
National Goal Leader: Association of State Educational Consultants for the Visually Impaired
c/o Indiana Department of Education, Division of Special Education
Room 229, State House
Indianapolis, IN 46204
317-232-0570
Contact: Sharon Knoth

GOAL 5: Array of Services
National Goal Leader: Council of Schools for the Blind
c/o Indiana School for the Blind
7725 North College Avenue
Indianapolis, IN 46240
317-253-1481
Contact: Dr. Michael Bina

GOAL 6: Assessment

National Goal Leader: The National Center for Vision and Child Development
The Lighthouse Inc.
111 East 59th Street
New York, NY 10022
212-821-9200
Contact: Dr. Mary Ann Lang

GOAL 7: Access to Instructional Materials

National Goal Leader: Association of Instructional Resource Centers for the Visually Handicapped
c/o Florida Instructional Materials Center
5002 North Lois Avenue
Tampa, FL 33614
813-872-5281
Contact: Suzanne Dalton

GOAL 8: Core Curriculum

National Goal Leader: Texas School for the Blind and Visually Impaired
1100 West 45th Street
Austin, TX 78757
512-454-8631
Contact: Dr. Phil Hatlen

ENDORSING ORGANIZATIONS

The organizations and agencies listed below have endorsed the National Agenda by signing the following statement:

> [Name of organization] endorses the *National Agenda for the Education of Children and Youths with Visual Impairments, Including Those with Multiple Disabilities.* Our organization will endeavor to work toward achieving its goals within the context of our professional associations with children and youths with visual impairments and their families.

National Organizations
American Council of the Blind
American Foundation for the Blind
American Printing House for the Blind
Association for Education and Rehabilitation of the Blind and Visually Impaired
Association for Instructional Resource Centers for Visually Handicapped Students
Blind Children's Fund
Choices for Children
Council for Exceptional Children
Delta Gamma Foundation
Descriptive Video Service
Hadley School for the Blind
Helen Keller National Center for Deaf-Blind Youths and Adults
Lions World Services for the Blind
National Accreditation Council for Agencies Serving the Blind and Visually Impaired
National Association for Parents of the Visually Impaired
National Industries for the Blind
National Marfan Foundation
National Organization for Albinism and Hypopigmentation
Rehabilitation Research and Training Center on Blindness and Low Vision

Specialized Schools
Alabama Institute for Deaf and Blind
Arizona State Schools for the Deaf and the Blind
California School for the Blind
Colorado School for the Deaf and the Blind
Florida School for the Deaf and the Blind
Georgia Academy for the Blind
Idaho School for the Deaf and the Blind
Illinois School for the Visually Impaired
Indiana School for the Blind

Iowa Braille and Sight Saving School
Kansas State School for the Blind
Lavelle School for the Blind, New York
Louisiana School for the Visually Impaired
Maryland School for the Blind
Michigan School for the Blind
Minnesota State Academy for the Blind
Mississippi School for the Blind
Missouri School for the Blind
Nebraska School for the Visually Handicapped
New Mexico School for the Visually Impaired
New York Institute for Special Education
Ohio State School for the Blind
Oregon School for the Blind
Overbrook School for the Blind
Parkview School, Oklahoma
Perkins School for the Blind, Massachusetts
Saint Joseph's School for the Blind, New Jersey
South Carolina School for the Deaf and the Blind
Tennessee School for the Blind
Texas School for the Blind and Visually Impaired
Utah Schools for the Deaf and the Blind
Virginia School for the Deaf and the Blind, Hampton
Virginia School for the Deaf and the Blind, Staunton
Washington State School for the Blind
West Virginia Schools for the Deaf and the Blind
Western Pennsylvania School for Blind Children
Wisconsin School for the Visually Handicapped

Multiservice Private and State Agencies
Anchor Center for Blind Children, Denver, CO
Blind Association of Western New York Visually Impaired Preschool, Amherst, NY
Blind Babies Foundation, San Francisco, CA
Blind Childrens Center, Los Angeles, CA
Blind Children's Learning Center, Santa Ana, CA
Braille Institute, Los Angeles, CA
Center for Blind and Visually Impaired Children, Milwaukee, WI
Center for the Visually Impaired, Atlanta, GA
Chicago Lighthouse for People Who Are Blind or Visually Impaired, Chicago, IL
Children's Center for the Visually Impaired, Kansas City, MO
Crotched Mountain Rehabilitation Center, Greenfield, NH
Dallas Services for Visually Impaired Children, Dallas, TX
Delco Blind/Sight Center, Chester, PA
Delta Gamma Center for Children with Visual Impairments, St. Louis, MO
Foundation for Blind Children, Phoenix, AZ
Foundation for the Junior Blind, Los Angeles, CA
Pittsburgh Vision Services, Pittsburgh, PA (formerly Greater Pittsburgh Guild for the Blind)
Helen Keller Services for the Blind, Brooklyn, NY
Jewish Guild for the Blind, New York, NY
The Lighthouse, Inc., New York, NY
Living Skills Center for the Visually Handicapped, San Pablo, CA

PennTech, Pennsylvania Department of Education, Harrisburg, PA
The Rehabilitation Center, New Haven, CT
Southern Access, Inc., Marietta, GA
Vision Associates, Orlando, FL
Vision Enrichment Services, Grand Rapids, MI

Local Education Agency Programs
Blount County Schools, Maryville, TN
Cannon County Schools, Woodbury, TN
Catholic Charities Education Services for Blind and Visually Impaired, Augusta, ME
Cheatham County Board of Education, Ashland City, TN
Charleston County School District, Charleston, SC
Columbia Regional Program: Vision Services, Portland, OR
Cumberland County Schools, Crossville, TN
DeKalb County Schools, Visually Impaired Program, Atlanta, GA
Grainger Board of Education, Rutledge, TN
Greeneville City School System, Greeneville, TN
Harriman City Schools, Harriman, TN
Hawkins County School System, Rogersville, TN
Hollow Rock-Bruceton Special School District, Bruceton, TN
Jackson-Madison County Schools, Jackson, TN
Johnson County Board of Education, Mountain City, TN
Lauderdale County Department of Special Education, Ripley, TN
Los Angeles Unified School District Program for Visually Impaired Students, Los Angeles, CA
Marshall County Board of Education, Lewisburg, TN
Memphis City Schools, Memphis, TN
Metropolitan Nashville Public Schools, Madison TN
Monroe County Schools, Madisonville, TN
New York City Public Schools, New York, NY
Oakridge Public Schools, Muskegon, MI
Overton County Schools Special Education, Livingston, TN
Scott County Schools, Huntsville, TN
Smith County School System, Carthage, TN
Special Education Service Agency, Anchorage, AK
Tennessee Infant-Parent Services School, Knoxville, TN
Trenton Special School District, Trenton, TN
Tyler D.C. Vision Program, Washington, D.C.
Vision Services Center, Bethesda, Maryland
Visually Impaired Preschool Services, Louisville, KY
Wilson County Special Education, Lebanon, TN

State Organizations, Departments of Education, and Other
Advocates and Parents of Oklahoma's Sight Impaired
Alamo Area Chapter, National Association for Parents of Visually Impaired
Atlantic Provinces Special Education Authority Resource Centre for the Visually Impaired, Nova Scotia,
  Canada
California Council of the Blind
California Low Incidence Disability Advisory Committee
California Transcribers and Educators for the Visually Handicapped
Colorado Department of Education
Connecticut Parents' Association for the Blind and Visually Impaired
Florida Department of Education, Division of Blind Services

Ho'opono Services for the Blind, Hawaii Department of Human Services
Iowa Bureau of Special Education
Maine State Division for the Blind and Visually Impaired
National Federation of the Blind of California
New York State Resource Center for the Visually Impaired
North Carolina Department of Public Instruction Exceptional Children's Support Team
Northern California Chapter, Association for Education and Rehabilitation of the Blind and Visually
    Impaired
Pennsylvania Council of the Blind
Tennessee State Department of Education
Texas Commission for the Blind
Texas Education Agency

Personnel Preparation Programs in Visual Impairment at Colleges and Universities
California State University at Los Angeles
Dominican College, New York
Florida State University
Hunter College, City University of New York
Michigan State University
Northern Illinois University
Pennsylvania College of Optometry
San Francisco State University
Texas Tech University
University of Arizona
University of Arkansas at Little Rock
University of North Dakota
University of Northern Colorado
University of Pittsburgh Vision Studies Program
University of South Carolina
Vanderbilt University, Tennessee
Western Michigan University

Low Vision Centers
Center for the Partially Sighted, Santa Monica, CA
Illinois Eye Institute, Chicago, IL
Low Vision Services, Utah Division of State Services for the Visually Handicapped, Salt Lake City, UT
Saint Mary Low Vision Center, Long Beach, CA
William Feinbloom Vision Rehabilitation Center, Philadelphia, PA

Many individuals, local chapters of national organizations, and manufacturers of assistive devices have endorsed the National Agenda. While these endorsements have been acknowledged, space restrictions preclude including them in this list.

OFFICE OF SPECIAL EDUCATION PROGRAMS (OSEP) POLICY STATEMENTS

TO: Chief State School Officers
FROM: Judith E. Heumann, Assistant Secretary
            Office of Special Education and Rehabilitative Services
            Thomas Hehir, Director
            Office of Special Education Programs
SUBJECT: Policy Guidance on Educating Blind and Visually Impaired Students

One of our highest priorities at the Office of Special Education and Rehabilitative Services (OSERS) is improving services for students with low incidence disabilities, particularly those with sensory deficits. On October 30, 1992, the Department published a Notice of Policy Guidance on Deaf Students Education Services[1] (Notice) to provide additional guidance to educators on the free appropriate public education (FAPE) requirements of Part B of the Individuals with Disabilities Education Act (Part B) and Section 504 of the Rehabilitation Act of 1973[2] as they relate to students who are deaf. In OSEP Memorandum 94-15, dated February 4, 1994, we clarified that the policy guidance in this Notice is equally applicable to all students with disabilities.

Nevertheless, it has come to our attention that services for some blind and visually impaired students are not appropriately addressing their unique educational and learning needs, particularly their needs for instruction in literacy, self-help skills, and orientation and mobility. We at OSERS are strongly committed to ensuring that our educational system takes the steps that are necessary to enable students who are blind or visually impaired to become productive and contributing citizens. Therefore, OSERS has determined that there is a need for additional guidance on the FAPE requirements of Part B as they relate to blind and visually impaired students. This guidance will provide some background information on blind and visually impaired students and discussion of their unique needs, and will identify the steps that educators can take in meeting their responsibilities under Part B to blind and visually impaired students.

---

[1] See 57 Reg. 49274 (Oct. 30, 1992).
[2] Section 504 of the Rehabilitation Act of 1973 (Section 504) prohibits discrimination on the basis of disability by recipients of federal financial assistance. The Department's regulations implementing Section 504, at 34 CFR Part 104, require recipients that operate public elementary and secondary education programs to provide appropriate educational services to disabled students. See 34 CFR SS104.33-104.36. Section 504 is enforced by the Department's Office for Civil Rights (OCR). The Americans with Disabilities Act of 1990 (ADA), Title II, prohibits discrimination on the basis of disability by state and local governments, whether or not they receive federal funds; OCR enforces Title II of the ADA as it relates to public elementary and secondary educational institutions and public libraries, and interprets the requirements of Title II of the ADA as consistent with those of Section 504. OCR officials have reviewed this guidance and find it to be consistent with recipients' obligations to provide FAPE to blind and visually impaired students under section 504 and Title II of the ADA.

We hope that the attached guidance is helpful to you and educators in your state as you implement educational programs for blind and visually impaired students. If there are any questions, or if further information is needed, please contact the contact person listed above or Dr. JoLeta Reynolds in the Office of Special Education Programs at (202) 205-5507.

Background

The population of students who receive services under Part B because of blindness or visual impairment is extremely diverse. These students display both a wide range of vision difficulties and adaptations to vision loss. The diversity that characterizes the student population is true of the population of blind and visually impaired persons in general. So far as degree of vision loss is concerned, the student population includes persons who are totally blind or persons with minimal light perception, as well as persons with high levels of functional vision, though less than the norm. For some students, visual impairment is their only disability; while others have one or more additional disabilities that will affect, to varying degrees, their learning and growth.

Identifying other characteristics of this diverse population is far more complex. This is because adaptations to vision loss vary greatly and are shaped by individual differences in areas such as intellectual abilities and family supports. Degree of vision loss, therefore, does not give a full understanding of how that loss affects learning. Students with similar degrees of vision loss may function very differently. A significant visual deficit can pose formidable obstacles for some students and far less formidable obstacles for others. However, regardless of the degree of the student's vision loss or the student's ability to adapt to that loss, there is general agreement that blind and visually impaired students must acquire the skills necessary to function in settings in which the majority of people have vision sufficient to enable them to read and write by using regular print as well as to move about in their environment with ease.

To state the obvious, children begin at a very young age to imitate the actions of others, particularly by imitating what they see others doing. Typically, learning is based on this principle. The challenge for educators of blind and visually impaired students in schools is how to teach their students to learn skills that sighted students typically acquire through vision, including how to read, write, compose, and obtain access to information contained in printed materials. We recognize that blind and visually impaired students have used a variety of methods to learn to read and write. For example, for reading purposes, some students use braille exclusively; others use large print or regular print with or without low vision aids. Still others use a combination of methods, including braille, large print, and low vision aids while others have sufficient functional vision to use regular print, although with considerable difficulty. In order to receive an appropriate education under Part B, unless a student who is blind or visually impaired has other disabilities that would inhibit his or her ability to learn to read, we believe that instruction in reading must be provided for blind and visually impaired students in the medium that is appropriate for their individual abilities and needs to enable them to learn to read effectively.

One of the most serious concerns voiced by parents of blind children and their advocates, and by adults who are blind or visually impaired as well, is that the number of students receiving instruction in braille has decreased significantly over the past several decades. As a result, these individuals believe that braille instruction is not being provided to some students for whom it may be appropriate. Braille has been a very effective reading and writing medium for many blind and visually impaired persons. In fact, data from a recent study demonstrate that blind and visually impaired adults who know braille are more likely to be employed than those who do not, suggesting a strong correlation between knowledge of braille and a person's ability to obtain future employment. The American Foundation for the Blind's Careers and Technology Information Bank, which lists 1,000 different jobs held by blind and visually impaired people, indicates that 85 percent of those who use braille as their primary method of reading are employed.[3]

---

[3]Study of Issues and Strategies toward Improving Employment of Blind and Visually Impaired Persons in Illinois, American Foundation for the Blind (March 1991).

Undoubtedly, there are numerous other benefits that individuals for whom braille instruction is appropriate would derive from knowledge of braille, particularly a heightened sense of self-esteem and self-worth that a student gains from the ability to read effectively.

Another significant concern voiced by parents of blind and visually impaired students and their advocates, as well as by many blind and visually impaired adults, is that these students are not receiving adequate instruction in orientation and mobility to address their individual needs. In some instances, it has been reported that these students do not even receive adequate evaluations of their needs for such instruction. The intent of Part B cannot be achieved fully if a blind or visually impaired student who needs instruction in orientation and mobility does not receive that instruction before completing his or her education.

I. Application of the Free Appropriate Public Education Requirements of Part B to Blind and Visually Impaired Students

Under Part B, each State and its public agencies must ensure that all children with specified disabilities have available to them a free appropriate public education (FAPE), and that the rights and projections of Part B are afforded to those students and their parents. FAPE includes, among other elements, special education and related services that are provided at no cost to parents under public supervision and direction, that meet State education standards and Part B requirements, that include preschool, elementary, or secondary school education in the State involved, and that are provided in conformity with an individualized education program (IEP).[4]

Before a student with a disability can receive special education and related services, a full and individual evaluation of the student's educational needs must be conducted in accordance with the requirements of 34 CFR S300.532.[5] Section 300.532 requires, among other factors, that the child be evaluated by a multidisciplinary team or group of persons, including at least one teacher or other specialist with knowledge in the area of suspected disability.[6] Thus, for blind or visually impaired students, an individual with knowledge of blindness and visual impairment would be an essential participant on this multidisciplinary team.

An assessment that meets the requirements of Part B must assess the child in all areas related to the suspected disability, including, if appropriate, "health, vision, hearing, social and emotional status, general intelligence, academic performance, communicative status, and motor abilities."[7] Assessments for blind and visually impaired students must evaluate the student in the areas listed above, as determined appropriate by the multidisciplinary team.

For example, an assessment of academic performance would include an assessment of the student's ability to master the skills necessary for literacy, including reading, reading comprehension, composition, and computing. If appropriate, an assessment of vision would include the nature and extent of the student's visual impairment and its effect on the student's ability to learn to read, write, and the instructional method or methods that would be appropriate to enable the student to learn the above skills. For the teaching of reading and composition, these methods could include braille, large print or regular print with or without low vision optical devices, or a combination of braille and print. A range of devices that utilize computer-generated speech could be helpful tools in the instruction of children who are blind or visually impaired. Because of the importance for some blind and visually impaired students of mastering the skills necessary to acquire information, additional assessments may be necessary to determine whether the student should receive specific instruction in listening skills. Possible assessments that could be considered for this purpose could include assessments of hearing, general intelligence, or communicative status. The student's need for instruction in orientation and mobility and the appropriate method or methods for acquiring this skill could also be assessed. As with other educational decisions, the results of the student's assessments must be

---

[4]20 U.S.C. S1412(2); 34 CFR S300.121; 20 U.S.C. S1401(a)(18) and 34 CFR S300.8

[5]34 CFR S300.531.

[6]*See* 34 CFR S300.532(e).

[7]*See* 34 CFR S300.531(f).

considered as the student's IEP[8] is developed, and the participants on the student's IEP team determine the specially designed instruction and related services to be provided to the student.

Under Part B, the public agency responsible for the student's education must initiate and conduct meetings to develop or review each student's IEP periodically, and if appropriate, revise its provisions. A meeting must be held for this purpose at least once a year.[9] Required participants at all IEP meetings include the child's teacher; an agency representative, who is qualified to provide or supervise the provision of special education; the parents, subject to certain limited exceptions; the child, if determined appropriate; and other individuals at the parent's or agency's discretion. If the IEP meeting occurs in connection with the child's initial placement in special education, the school district must ensure the participation of evaluation personnel, unless the child's teacher or public agency representative or some other person at the meeting is knowledgeable about the evaluation procedures used with the child and the results of those procedures.[10]

Each student's IEP must contain, among other components, a statement of annual goals including short-term objectives, the specific special education and related services to be provided to the student and the extent that the student will be able to participate in regular educational programs, and a statement of needed transition services under certain circumstances.[11] To ensure that blind and visually impaired students receive adequate instruction in the skills necessary to become literate, IEP teams must ensure that the instructional time that is allocated is appropriate for the required instruction or service.[12] For a student to become literate in braille, systematic and regular instruction from knowledgeable and trained personnel is essential. Likewise, for students with low vision, instruction in the utilization of remaining vision and in the effective use of low vision aids requires regular and intensive intervention from appropriately trained personnel.

In all instances, IEP teams must consider how to address the needs of blind and visually impaired students for the skills necessary to achieve literacy. For students who are blind or for students with a minimal amount of residual vision, it is probable that braille will be the primary instructional method for teaching the student to learn to read. Therefore, for blind students and for students with a minimal amount of residual vision, braille should be considered as the primary reading method, unless the student has a disability in addition to blindness that would make it difficult for the student to use his or her hands or would otherwise adversely affect the student's ability to learn to read. In developing IEPs for other students with low vision, IEP teams should not assume that instruction in braille would not be appropriate merely because the student has some useful vision. While IEP teams are not required to consider the need for braille instruction for every student with a visual impairment who is eligible for services under Part B, IEP teams may not fail to consider braille instruction for students for whom it may be appropriate. This consideration must occur despite factors such as shortages or unavailability of trained personnel to provide braille instruction, the ability of audiotapes and computers to provide blind and visually impaired persons with ready access to printed textbooks and materials, or the amount of time needed to provide a student with sufficient and regular instruction to attain proficiency in braille.

IEP teams also must select the method or methods for teaching blind and visually impaired students how to write and compose. Students whose appropriate reading medium is braille may benefit from using braille for these purposes. Alternatively, in addition to braille, they may benefit from using a personal computer with speech output for composition. Therefore, IEP teams must make individual determinations about the needs of blind and visually impaired students for instruction in writing and composition, and must include effective methods for teaching writing and composition in the IEPs of those students for whom instruction in this area is determined to be appropriate.

---

[8]The IEP is the written document that contains the statement for a disabled student of the program of specialized instruction and related services to be provided to a student. 34 SS300.340-300.350.

[9]20 U.S.C. S1414(a) (5) and 34 CFR S330.343(d).

[10]34 CFR S300.344.

[11]34 CFR S300.346.

[12]Appendix C to 34 CFR Part 300 (question 51).

In addition to mastering the skills taught to all students, blind and visually impaired students must receive instruction in the skills necessary to acquire information, particularly because braille or large print documents frequently cannot be made accessible to them in a timely manner. The skills that could be taught to accomplish this include recordings that utilize compressed speech, personal computers with speech output, and optical scanners with speech output. As determined appropriate, use of these devices and methods would be considered on an individual basis. In appropriate situations, one or more of these devices could be used to supplement braille instruction for students for whom braille is the primary reading medium, or to supplement print or large print for students using print as their primary reading medium. In rare instances, methods for acquiring information could be used in place of braille or print for students who, by reason of other disabilities, cannot be taught to read.

To ensure that IEPs for blind and visually impaired students address their specific needs effectively, the following unique needs should be considered as IEPs for these students are developed:

- Skills necessary to attain literacy in reading and writing, including appropriate instructional methods.
- Skills for acquiring information, including appropriate use of technological devices and services.
- Orientation and Mobility Instruction.
- Social Interaction Skills.
- Transition Services Needs.
- Recreation.
- Career Education.

This list is not intended to be exhaustive. Participants on IEP teams could determine that it would be appropriate to consider an individual student's needs for other skills, in addition to the skills listed above. Therefore, in making decisions about the educational programs for blind and visually impaired students, IEP teams must consider the full range of skills necessary to enable these students to learn effectively.

II. Least Restrictive Environment and Placement Requirements

Part B requires States to have procedures for assuring that, to the maximum extent appropriate, students with disabilities are educated with students who are not disabled, and that special classes, separate schooling, or other removal of students with disabilities from the regular education environment occurs only when the nature or severity of the disability is such that education in regular classes with the use of supplementary aids and services cannot be achieved satisfactorily.[13] This requirement is known as the least restrictive environment (LRE) requirement.

Recognizing that the regular classroom may not be the LRE placement for every disabled student, the Part B regulations require public agencies to make available a continuum of alternative placements, or a range of placement options, to meet the needs of students with disabilities for special education and related services. The options on this continuum, which include regular classes, special classes, separate schools, and instruction in hospitals and institutions, must be made available to the extent necessary to implement the IEP of each disabled student.[14]

Part B requires that each child's placement must be based on his or her IEP.[15] Thus, it is the special education and related services set out in each student's IEP that constitute the basis for the placement decision. That is why placement determination cannot be made before a student's IEP is developed. Rather, it is the special education and related services set out in the student's IEP that must constitute the basis for the placement decision. After the IEP of a blind or visually impaired student is developed, the placement determination must be made consistent with the special education and related services reflected in the student's IEP. In addition, the potential harmful effect of the placement on the visually impaired student or

---

[13]20 U.S.C. S1412(5)(B); 34 CFR S300.550(b).

[14]*See* 34 CFR SS300.551 and 300.552(b).

[15]*See* 34 CFR S300.552(a)(2). That regulation requires that each child's placement is determined at least annually, is based on his or her IEP, and is in the school or facility as close as possible to the child's home. 34 CFR S300.552(a)(1)–(3). Further, unless a disabled student's IEP requires another arrangement, the student must be educated in the school or facility that he or she would attend if not disabled. 34 CFR S300.552(c).

the quality of services he or she needs must be considered in determining the LRE.[16] The overriding rule in placement is that each student's placement must be determined on an individual basis.[17] As in other situations, placements of blind and visually impaired students may not be based solely on factors such as category of disability, severity of disability, configuration of delivery system, availability of educational or related services, availability of space, or administrative convenience.

In addition to the Part B requirements applicable to placement in the LRE, Part B requires that each student's placement decision be made by a "group of persons, including persons knowledgeable about the child, the meaning of evaluation data, and placement options."[18] While Part B does not explicitly require the participation of the child's parent on this placement team, many States include parents in the group of persons that makes placement decisions. It is also important to emphasize that parents of blind and visually impaired students, through their participation on the student's IEP team, can play a critical role in ensuring that the student's unique needs are appropriately addressed. Public agencies and parent information centers should take steps to ensure that parents are fully informed about the instructional media that are available to address the unique needs arising from the student's visual impairment.

In implementing Part B's LRE requirements, in some instances, place decisions are inappropriately made before IEPs that address a child's unique needs are developed. Determinations of appropriate special education and related services for blind and visually impaired students must be made through the IEP process, and must examine the development of skills necessary to address the effects of blindness or low vision on the student's ability to learn and to access the curriculum. Since Part B requires that each child's placement be based on his or her IEP, making placement decisions before a student's IEP is developed is a practice that violates Part B and could result in the denial of FAPE in the LRE.

Still, in other instances, some students have been inappropriately placed in the regular classroom although it has been determined that their IEPs cannot be appropriately implemented in the regular classroom even with the necessary supplementary aids and supports. In these situations, the nature of the student's disability and individual needs could make it appropriate for the student to be placed in a setting outside of the regular educational environment in order to ensure that the student's IEP is satisfactorily implemented. By contrast, there are other instances where some blind and visually impaired students have been inappropriately placed in settings other than the regular educational environment, even though their IEPs could have been implemented satisfactorily in the regular classroom with the provision of supplementary aids and services. As is true for all educational decisions under Part B, the above concerns about the misapplication of the LRE requirements underscore the importance of making individual placement determinations based on each student's unique abilities and needs.

In making placement determination, it is essential that placement teams consider the full range of placement options for blind and visually impaired students. The following are some examples of placement options that could be considered:

- Placement in a regular classroom with needed support services provided in that classroom by an itinerant teacher or by a special teacher assigned to that school.
- Placement in the regular classroom with services outside the classroom by an itinerant teacher or by a special teacher assigned to that school.
- Placement in a self-contained classroom in a regular school.
- Placement in a special school with residential option.

III. Procedural Safeguards

Part B also requires that public agencies afford parents a range of procedural safeguards. These include giving parents written notice a reasonable time before a public agency proposes to initiate, or change, the identification, evaluation, educational placement of the child, or the provision of a free appropriate public education to the child. This notice to parents must include a description of the action proposed, or refused,

---

[16]34 CFR S300.552(d).

[17]34 CFR S300.552 and Note 1.

[18]34 CFR S300.533(a) (3).

by the agency, an explanation of why the agency proposes, or refuses, to take the action, and a description of any options the agency considered and the reasons why those options were rejected.[19] The requirement to provide a description of any option considered includes a description of the types of placements that were actually considered, for example, regular class placement with needed support services, regular classroom with pull-out services; and the reasons why these placement options were rejected. Providing this kind of information to parents will enable them to play a more knowledgeable and informed role in the education of their children. Part B affords parents and public educational agencies the right to initiate an impartial due process hearing on any matter regarding the identification, evaluation, or educational placement of the child, or the provision of a free appropriate public education to the child.[20]

Disagreements between parents and public agencies over issues such as the extent that braille instruction should be included in a student's IEP and the educational setting in which the child's IEP should be implemented are examples of some of the matters that can be the subject of a Part B due process hearing. Since many State procedures call for mediation before resorting to formal due process procedures, issues that can be the subject of a Part B due process hearing also can be addressed through mediation if the State has such as a process, or through other alternative dispute resolution mechanisms. We strongly encourage alternative dispute resolution without a need to resort to due process and informing parents about such procedures. Public agencies also need to inform parents of blind and visually impaired students of their right to initiate a Part B due process hearing when agreement cannot be reached on important educational decisions.[21]

---

[19] *See* 34 CFR S300.504(a) and 300.505(a) (2)–(4).

[20] *See* 20 U.S.C. S1415(b) (1) (E) and 34 CFR S300.506(a).

[21] [In the 1997 reauthorization of the Individuals with Disabilities Education Act, Congress added the following provision: "The IEP Team shall . . . in the case of a child who is blind or visually impaired, provide for instruction in Braille and the use of Braille unless the IEP Team determines, after an evaluation of the child's reading and writing skills, needs, and appropriate reading and writing media (including an evaluation of the child's future needs for instruction in Braille or the use of Braille), that instruction in Braille or the use of Braille is not appropriate for the child." *See* 20 U.S.C. S1414 (d) (3) (B) (iii). *Eds.*]

About the Editors

Anne L. Corn, Ed.D., is Professor of Special Education, Ophthalmology and Visual Sciences, Vanderbilt University, Nashville, Tennessee, where she is also coordinator of the personnel preparation program in visual disabilities at Peabody College of Vanderbilt University. The winner in 1994 of the AER [Association for Education and Rehabilitation of the Blind and Visually Impaired] Division 7 (Low Vision) Award for Contributions to Literature and Research and in 1990 of the Distinguished Service Award, Low Vision Section of the American Optometric Association, she is the author of numerous books, articles, and other publications and a frequent speaker at national and international conferences. Dr. Corn is past president of the Division on Visual Handicaps of the Council for Exceptional Children and past chair of AER's Division 17 (Personnel Preparation). She was also the chair of the Steering Committee of the National Agenda for the Education of Children and Youths with Visual Impairments, Including Those with Multiple Disabilities.

Kathleen Mary Huebner, Ph.D., is Associate Professor and Assistant Dean of Graduate Studies, Institute for the Visually Impaired, Pennsylvania College of Optometry in Philadelphia. Previously, she was Director of the National Program Associates Department, Director of the AFB Deaf-Blind Project, and National Consultant in Education at the American Foundation for the Blind. She also directed the Graduate Teacher Training Program at the State University of New York at Geneseo. She is a former instructor of individuals with visual impairments and an orientation and mobility specialist. Dr. Huebner has co-authored and edited several books, including the award-winning *Hand in Hand* series from AFB Press, as well as numerous articles on services for individuals who are visually impaired. She is a frequent presenter and consultant working with schools, teacher training programs, parent organizations, and government agencies throughout the nation and abroad on topics related to blindness and multiple impairments. Dr. Huebner was a member of the original Steering Committee of the National Agenda and continues to serve on the Advisory Board.